"Twice Ambushed"

Horror Stories of the Veterans Administration

Charles L. Pemberton Sr., Ph. D.

Twice Ambushed

I wish to dedicate *"Twice Ambushed Horror Stories of the Veterans Administration"* to every American military veteran who has had to deal with the Veterans Administration.

May God bless the "protectors" of our freedom.

Special Thanks to:

Darlena Ricketts M.S. - Editing

Mary Pemberton A.S. – Editing

CaSanda L. Bevis B.A. - Editing

Lola Wandrey – Proofreading

Edgard Sanchez – Front cover photo

Jimmy Pemberton – Poem

Twice Ambushed

Additional copies may be ordered from:

Major bookstores

Amazon. Com

Or

Dr. C. L. Pemberton Sr.
P.O. Box 24
Homeland, Fl. 33847

Tel. 863-602-3423

Contents

"Our Veterans Are Being Abused" - - - - - - - - - - - - - 5

Introduction - 7

Chapter 1 - - First Time Soldier - - - - - - - - - - - - - 14

Chapter 2 - - Years of Pain - - - - - - - - - - - - - - - - - 22

Chapter 3 - - The System - - - - — - - - - - - - - - - - - -28

Chapter 4 - - Lost Time - - - - - - - - - - - — - - - - - - - 37

Chapter 5 - - Hearing at Bay Pines - - - - - - - - - - - - 47

Chapter 6 - - Assistance Requested - - - - - - - - - - - 57

Chapter 7 - - U.S. Congressman Putnam - - - - - - - 65

Chapter 8 - - Vanishing Records - - - - - - - - - - - - - -71

Chapter 9 - - Forty-Five Years later - - - - - - - - - - - 77

Chapter 10 - - Second Ambush - - - - - - - - - - - - - - - 88

Chapter 11- - Bartow Regional Hospital- - - -- - - - - 96

Chapter 12 - - The Battle Rages - - - - - - - - - - - - - - 103

Chapter 13 - - Run-Around Continues - - - - - - - - - 119

Chapter 14 - - Horror Stories - - - - - - - - - - - - - - - - 128

Chapter 15 - - Memphis - - - - - - - - - - - - - - - - - - - 141

Chapter 16 - - Re-connected - - - - - - - - - - - - - - - - 150

Chapter 17 - - Conclusion - - - - - - - - - - - - - - - - - 157

"Our Veterans Are Being Abused"

We have millions of veterans who faithfully served.
Many are getting something
they never deserved.

Those who faithfully made
a commitment to the U.S. . . . .
Are now coping with a lot of
After duty stress

Many ask themselves; "Where did I go wrong?"
Are living in a country where
They feel they don't belong.

Many of them are being tossed around and discarded.
It was decades ago when much of this started.

The government set up its own kind of institution.
They decided to call it; "The Veterans Administration."

However, this administration has inflated many costs.
They have no idea of how many
lives have been lost.

Many veterans with problems, don't know
how to cope. Too many ends in suicide,
after they lost all sense of hope.

We need to encourage our government
to focus its attention.
*They need to get moving into **the Right Direction***

We need to give our veterans a heart of appreciation.
Let's offer them true hope and sincere dedication.

Twice Ambushed

Let's reach out to offer them hope and peace of mind.
Let's be there for them,
when they need help next time!

Our veterans have been our defense and foundation.
Without them, we've lost a big part of this nation!

By Jim Pemberton
Graham, Washington

"There is a way that seem right, but the end leads to destruction" (Prov. 14:12 NIV).

This Proverb is very fitting for this situation.

Introduction

"Twice Ambushed" is about a young man who served his country, as a soldier, in the U.S. Army. It was during the time of the Vietnam War. Returning home, he had escaped the effects of Post-Traumatic-Stress-Syndrome while on active duty. Certainly, he was not expected to have to endure excessive stress at the hands of the Veterans Administration. What should have been an easy encounter has lasted over forty years. This has created an unbelievable stress level that would have taken many good men out.

There are many people and businesses that try to show their appreciation to the veteran. For this, most veterans are thankful. Having said this, I feel there is one that should be mentioned with gratitude.

Some businesses extend a 10% discount to veterans which may be a marketing tactic. To stay in business a product is sold at a 400% or more markup. There are a large number of veterans in America and to offer a 10% discount just seems like good business. It helps to build the store's clientele.

Dolly Parton's "Dollywood" in Pigeon Forge, Tennessee does more to show their appreciation to the veteran than any other place I have encountered.

I have vacationed at Dollywood with my family about four times and each time I asked for a veteran's discount. A large discount was given to every member of my family. For this, a greater appreciation and respect for Dolly Parton has grown.

Other businesses may show their appreciation as

best as they can and for this we veterans are grateful.

Most Americans are not aware of the greatest problem encountered by many veterans. It is the Veterans Administration. This organization is responsible to assist veterans reacclimating back into society. In many cases it is their number one enemy.

The problems in the Veterans Administration have reached the level that the welfare of many veterans are affected.

The veterans encounter with the Veterans Administration exacerbates their stress level to the point of many committing suicide. For some it is the memory of war with others it is the isolation created by this monstrous system.

It is easy to research the horrible atrocities that happen within the Veterans Administration. One can simply google on their computer, "Horrible stories of the Veterans Administration."

There are so many stories of inefficiency throughout most of their health care facilities. Many cases led to the death of some veterans.

Another place to research "horrible stories" is within Veterans Organizations such as: The American Legion, Disable American Veterans, Wounded Warriors, and Veterans of Foreign Wars. The vets have their stories, and many are shocking. Any interested researcher will have to prepare themselves mentally for some disgusting stories.

After two claim attempts with the Veterans

Administration, the author attempts to enlighten the reader of the gross negligence within that organization. One such claim has been ongoing for over forty years.

An attempt to maneuver through the system started in 1976 when a service-connected disability claim was filed by the author. A subsequent second claim was filed in 2010 for "error in judgment" after being a patient at James A. Haley Hospital in Tampa, Florida turned into a nightmare.

Many Americans believe that veterans are being taken care of. That is far from the truth. With patriotism being higher than it has been in many years, there is a misconception that the veteran is being taken care of. The truth of the matter is, that concept is far from the truth.

People are programmed to "Thank a vet" for their service and some organizations are involved in building houses for disabled vets. It seems like the veteran is being looked out for in our society and this is commendable. However, there is a very high percentage of veterans that are homeless and denied health care.

Many veterans return home with disabilities that affect them for the rest of their lives. These disabilities occur while defending the freedom of each American.

The Veterans Administration is supposed to be there for the returning veteran to assist him/her in obtaining medical treatment and help with special needs that they bring home with them. Some of their special needs are long-term, and many will have to be dealt with for a long time.

Some returning troops, who are injured while in the military, are required to endure unbelievable resistance at the hands of the Veterans Administration.

Much of the information in this book is not commonly known by our society.

Large sums of monies are being spent by the government on propaganda tactics to "brain wash" it's citizenry. It seems to be working, as a result most Americans believe our veterans are well taken care of.

"Twice Ambushed" uncovers deceit and tactics used by the Veterans Administration that should be absolutely appalling to every American who has an ounce of patriotism. Tactics such as: stalling, destruction of records, burying incidents in huge stacks of records, and cover-ups to delay claims are common occurrences within this organization.

In many cases the Veteran will die before receiving proper treatment and in other cases veterans are denied disabilities claims that they rightly deserve.

Research shows that the percentage of veterans who receive benefits are much smaller than those who are denied. A large number of veterans who make claims for disabilities run into a brick wall. For many, it is so overwhelming.

This book reveals how the author had appeal after appeal denied at least fifteen times. The same claim has been ongoing for over forty years. Each appeal to the *Board of Veterans Appeals* usually took from one to five years. The *Board of Veterans Appeal* can be compared to the Federal Supreme Court.

Once a denial of a claim has been made at the local Veterans Administration it can be appealed to the Veterans Appeals Board in Washington, D.C.

Most veterans return to civilian life believing the V.A. has their backs. Only a few veterans collect copies of their files, especially health records. The reason for this neglect is because they have such confidence in the Veterans Administration's ability to safeguard records. This confidence is the result of the Veterans Administration convincing veterans that they are good custodians of records.

There are many dedicated and knowledgeable medical personnel that serve returning veterans. At times, it probably seems like a "thankless" job for many. It is not the intention of this expose' to attack the medical personnel and their tireless efforts who work in the medical facilities.

Most of the incompetence lies within the administrative personnel who will go to great lengths to cover up mistakes made in these facilities.

The veteran deserves to be treated with respect by the Veterans Administration. They need to do more than just say "thank you." Every veteran has taken an oath to defend the United States against its enemies, both foreign and domestic. That oath is a commitment. This commitment requires the giving of their life, if necessary. Since the U.S.A. operates on an all-volunteer military, recruiters have to locate and enlist young patriotic people who are willing to give their lives for a country they love.

This same patriotic commitment should exist in the Veterans Administration. Instead, it has become a part of the world of politics. Recently some changes have been made at the helm of the Veterans Administration, however, change is not reaching the level that needs it. The President of the United States can keep changing the man at the top but if change does not affect the veteran then the system will remain ineffective.

It is said by many veterans that the V. A. Medical Care System "affords a veteran a second chance to give his/her life for their country."

What do you say Mr./Ms. politician? *Can you hear veterans are screaming? Change needs to be in their favor.*

Research could not produce an all-inclusive expose' due to the magnitude of the system. However, overwhelming evidence is presented to support the claim that the Veterans Administration is guilty of committing some of the greatest atrocities known to the veteran. The most common technique used by them is: stalling, denying, and misplacing records, in hopes that the claimant will eventually die. Once the veteran dies, the claim will go away.

This book needs to find itself in the hands of politicians, government leaders, and any person willing to do whatever it takes to make a change.

It is the goal of this author to enlighten the reader to the plight of the veteran and hopefully, as a result it will affect change for our returning "heroes."

Chapter One: First Time Soldier

I was known as "Charlie" where I grew-up in Henderson County, Kentucky. In 1962, I became seventeen. With four brothers and a sister ahead of me and two brothers and a sister behind me I grew up in a family full of patriotism. In my family, joining the military was just something the boys of the family did.

As a kid I saw my older brothers come home wearing the uniform of the branch of military that they were serving. Some enlisted in the Army and some enlisted in the Air Force. The sight of them would cause me to swell with pride. I thought, "someday, I will wear one." With pride I would show-off my brothers to my friends and all the time thinking, "someday, I will wear a uniform." The more I showed-off my brothers the more anxious I was for my time to come. It grew harder and harder to wait for my seventeenth birthday.

Finally, Sgt. Hopkins, the recruiting sergeant, showed up at my house. He was the local recruiter that had enlisted my brothers and he had been keeping a close eye on my birthday. The day that I had so anxiously waited for had finally arrived.

Sgt. Hopkins completed all the necessary paper work and bought me a bus ticket to the U.S. Army Induction Center in Louisville, Kentucky.

With emotions running rampant, I boarded the bus in Henderson, Kentucky. The thoughts of leaving my mother and younger siblings would not leave me. I knew life was taking a new course and it was leading me away from my home. Things would change forever.

As the bus pulled out of the station I waved good-bye to my mother and siblings. As the bus put distance between me and my family, the last thing I saw was tears streaming down my mother's cheeks. Suddenly, I felt my eyes began to tear up. Sixty-years have passed, my mother, five brothers and two sisters have deceased, and yet I have not been able to erase that memory from my mind.

At the U.S. Army induction station in Louisville, Kentucky, I was given several written examinations. I achieved the required score on the written examinations and continue to the health physical which was the last to take place.

It was the military medical personnel's responsibility to determine whether a person could medically and psychologically rise to a level to meet the strenuous training of a soldier. It was found that I met all the requirements and absolutely no health issues were found.

Flat feet would be a disqualifying factor and usually prevented a person from serving in the military. A couple of years later, this would become an issue.

During the three days at the induction station I finished all necessary tests and physicals. The last event to take place was taking the "oath of a soldier." This was really thought provoking. I had to swear that I would defend the Constitution of the United States against both foreign and domestic enemies, even if to the point of death. That was much for a seventeen-year-old to take in.

My first assignment was Company D, 13th Battalion, 2nd Training Brigade at Fort Knox, Kentucky for BCT (Basic combat training). The next eight weeks would include rigorous physical training. During Basic training, the soldiers would march everywhere they went. Many times, this included a fifteen-mile march with a ninety-pound pack of field gear on your back. The rifle range, where we qualified with weapons, were many miles from the barracks.

There are two distinct hills at Fort Knox that every soldier had to march up during basic training. One is called "Misery" and the other one called "Agony." They are on the route that the "full field march" took. The platoon marched over them several times. At the time, most soldiers did not realize the damage that could be done to their feet.

After completion of basic training, I was assigned to Company C, 6th Battalion, 2nd training Brigade at Fort Knox, Kentucky, as permanent party. In this assignment, I was given a duty MOS (Military Occupation Specialty) of 640 (light vehicle driver).

During my time at Fort Knox I was sent TDY (Temporary Duty Yonder) to Fort Lee, Virginia for two months. Duty assigned to me required prolonged standing, some pain was felt in my feet during this time. However, the pain level was tolerable. For the next year, while being stationed in the United States, I continued to work as a light vehicle driver. Driving a vehicle did not require prolong standing so most of the time the pain level continued to be tolerable.

The Cuban Crisis unfolded in October 1962, I had been in the military for just four months. During the crisis, the announcement was made that the likelihood of the U.S. going to war with the Soviet Union was great. Later it was discovered that the United States had come closer to a nuclear war than ever before in history. This was a lot of information for a seventeen-year-old to process.

After being assigned to Fort Knox, Kentucky for fourteen months, orders came down for a duty assignment in Germany. A country boy who had barely turned eighteen was now being sent halfway around the world. Unimaginable at the time, however, in retrospect it was a life changer.

In 1964 the Viet-Nam War was escalating in that part of the world. President Johnson ordered 500,000 troops into South Viet-Nam. Before it was over 55,000 young American men and women lost their lives. Thousands came home maimed, needing the services of the Veterans Administration.

Being in Germany was a new experience and every assignment was approached with much anticipation.

Severe foot pain shows up - While on active duty in Germany, the Cold War was brewing with the Soviet Union. Physical training became an everyday practice. I began to suffer extreme pain in my feet. After making several trips on sick call at the dispensary, in Benjamin Franklin Village, Mannheim, Germany, I was sent to the military hospital in Heidelberg, Germany.

Several medical tests were administered, and the doctor said their findings indicated the joints in my ankles were spreading and there was no treatment available at that time. The only possible treatment available was to treat the pain. So, this was the beginning of many years of pain management and appointments to health professionals without results.

A medical profile was issued - The military doctor (a podiatrist) signed a medical profile which stated:

"patient could not be assigned duties such as: guard duty, KP, and PT. It further stated that patient could not wear combat boots. Special low-quarters were to be made at the quartermaster. Patient would need to sit at least fifteen minutes out of every hour."

The doctor said this was a long-term condition and had probably started when I was a small boy. The doctor suggested initiating a medical discharge without compensation. Compensation would not be offered because he claimed the condition was not an injury caused while serving in the U.S. Army. This was the beginning of a cover-up.

Two *arguments should have been considered.*

(1) The condition was not discovered in the initial enlistment physical.

(2) If by chance the condition did exist prior to the enlistment, the strenuous requirements during basic training had aggravated the situation. The treatment done at the military hospital established a treatment

record which should have been a part of the medical records.

A medical discharge is offered -The attending physician suggested that a medical discharge should be considered. A medical discharge could have long-term civilian ramification. Certain civilian employment could be affected. I had been entertaining the idea of becoming a police officer in civilian life and a medical discharge could affect that possibility.

The physician left the decision up to me. I decided against a medical discharge since there were only six months left in my enlistment. The "medical profile" allowed some discretion in everyday duties. In the months ahead, the active duty enlistment was finished, and I was sent home.

American Sentiment – By the time I arrived home the Vietnam war was full blown. People like Jane Fonda were trying to destroy American patriotism. Soon anti-Americanism was surging and demonstrations against the war was going strong. Everyone perceived to be a part of the war was targeted. The hatred against the American soldier was at an all-time high. Most veterans did not feel comfortable admitting that they had served, whether it was in Vietnam or anywhere else. With the American sentiment being as it was most returning veterans did not want anything to do with the military or with the Veterans Administration.

Soon after I was separated from the army I contacted the Veterans Administration asking about filing a disability claim. The Veterans Administration responded so negative toward the returning veterans that many stayed away from them. Their response to my inquiry was pretty much, "we are not here to give you welfare."

Patriotism had compelled many to enlist in the U.S. military, and it also kept them from seeking what was perceived as a handout.

The American sentiment was at an all-time low. Many soldiers/veterans were spit on and rocks were thrown at them during the Vietnam War years (1964-1973). It took years for the social rife to heal. As a result, many veterans developed non-combat PTSD. What seemed like the best plan of action for many veterans was just not talk about the military. This seemed to just exacerbate the problem.

Ten years later – Ten years after separation from active duty, the pain level had forced me to be selective in employment careers.

In 1975 the word was starting to circulate that the American sentiment was changing and as a result the Veterans Administration was beginning to assist veterans.

This information was well received by many and the idea of filing a disability claim surfaced again. A claim was filed for disability and soon I was notified that no military health records existed on me.

Supposedly all my health records had "disappeared. This was the beginning of a forty-three- year saga with the Veterans Administration. It continues even today. When the first disability claim was filed I was very naïve and approached the filing of the claim with high expectations. It was impossible to realize the level of ruthlessness and deceit that was aimed at veterans. Even today it is unimaginable for most people to believe that the veterans of the good ole U.S.A. could be treated so badly.

Chapter Two: Years of Pain

After the initial disability claim was filed it took over a year for the VA to respond. The first letter notified me that the claim had been denied. It came as no real surprise since most veteran's claims are denied on the first submission.

The reason given for the denial was the surprise. It stated that they could not confirm treatment for claimed injury. It also stated they could not locate any of my health records for the time I was in the service. The excuse given was a fire had swept through the Army Records Center in 1973 and the possibility existed that my health records had been destroyed.

Immediately, I filed an appeal. The appeal included an explanation that I had been treated several times while stationed in Germany. The treatment took place at a U.S. military hospital in Heidelberg, Germany.

A denial of the appeal arrived several months later. I was soon overcome with a feeling of being deserted by the Veterans Administration. I had rocks thrown at me and spit upon, while serving in the "Cold war." Now I felt they were playing mind games with me. I believed that I had been there when my country needed me but now they discarded me as you would an old rag.

Pain management became a daily routine. Only when I was not required to stand for long periods of time was the pain manageable. Pain management included using special arches in my shoes and not standing for prolonged periods of time.

McDonnel Aircraft Company in St. Louis, Missouri. had a contract with the federal government to train veterans. During training, the pay was only half of the normal pay scale. Tests were administered to the veteran to qualify him/her for different positions that were available. Most veterans were trained in the areas of sheet metal, quality control, or mechanics. I applied and was assigned to the quality control school. It lasted for six weeks and the training included the use of inspection tools and the reading of blueprints.

I had no trouble in fulfilling the responsibilities because the training did not require a person to stand for long periods of time. After the training, I was assigned to work in the receiving department and most of this work was done while sitting at a work table.

After a couple of years, at the request of my brother, I sent an application to Boeing Aircraft Company in Seattle, Washington. Boeing offered me a position as a production controller.

This job did not require long periods of standing except for at times. When it was necessary to stand for long periods of time the pain became all too real again.

For the next few years several appointments were made to see a podiatrist. On a couple of occasions, special arches were ordered as inserts. These treatments did not relieve the pain and at times, they increased the pain level.

Boeing has a massive layoff - After three years of employment with this company, Boeing encountered a work slowdown. It resulted in the lay-off of 75,000 employees. At this time, I had to start job hunting all over again.

It became a struggle over the next few years to continue working and earning a living for my family. Over the next ten years many specialists were consulted as I sought help in finding help with my feet problems. Most of the time, the doctors would prescribe arch supports, however, this did not deal with the pain I was suffering.

At the end of each work shift the pain was so intense that I would hobble out to the parking lot to my vehicle. Upon arriving home, the ritual consisted of soaking my feet in hot salt water for about an hour. This would give some relief. Many times, the level of pain was at unbearable levels.

The first seven years of married life we lived in Missouri, Washington, Indiana, and Kentucky. I kept seeking jobs that did not require having to stand for long periods of time. After a few years of moving from one state to another I eventually moved to Florida. This move was brought on so that I could attend college. Upon enrollment at Southeastern University in Lakeland, Florida, I was accepted into their summer session. As a student, I had to support my family, so it required me to work. I continued to seek a job that didn't require long term standing. The jobs that were available with this stipulation were few and paid very little.

After graduating from college, the next 32 years I worked as a teacher and pastor. Teaching provided an income to provide for my family. However, some administrators thought that not being able to stand long term diminished my teaching skills.

The struggle continues - Pain management became a major effort during the years that followed. I continued to believe that the army was responsible for the break-down of my feet which caused the suffering.

Because of the Vietnam War and the American sentiment, most veterans just suffered in silence. Many that needed help felt like they had been betrayed by the system.

Standing for hours teaching in the classroom brought back extreme pain at an unbearable level. In the afternoons it was common practice to fall across a bed for a couple of hours from extreme exhaustion.

Visits to podiatrists became routine for the next several years. Their prescription was usually the same; arch supports and stay off the feet as much as possible.

One podiatrist, who was also a surgeon, suggested surgery as a possibility. I decided that option would have to wait for a while. That suggestion would be considered only if there was no other way.

Another podiatrist suggested a "Richie brace." It was agreed upon and this plan of action was initiated. Within about a month the "Richie brace" was made. The brace rubbed sores on the back of my leg and when I asked the podiatrist if an adjustment was available for the brace, the standard answer was "no, get use to it"

Still no solution to my claim – After forty years the claim is no closer to a fair verdict. Request after request for assistance has been sent to the Department of Defense, several U.S. Senators, Congressmen, and different service organizations. Just about anyone who has authority received a letter from me asking for their assistance.

DAV Organization – Recently, a solicitation from the Disabled American Veterans Organization was mailed out. It was asking for a contribution to help support their programs. Their claim to helping veterans appeared somewhat misleading.

The title of the brochure stated: ***Guide a Vet to DAV Service Programs.*** The content stated;

"When you hear of veterans coming home ill and injured from their service in the armed forces, does the question, "How can I help?" come to mind? If so, DAV has your answer.

Veterans and their families need to know help is there when they need it. DAV provides the resources to address needs like help with claims for disability benefits and compensation, transportation to medical appointments, and so much more."

DAV's National Service Program – provides Transition Service Officers (TSOs) who provide a critical bridge as our troops leave military service and return to civilian life. TSOs counsel these service members on the benefits they have earned as veterans.

Judicial Appeals — DAV provides *pro bono* representation for veterans seeking review in the U.S. Court of Appeals for veterans claims to identify cases where claims have been improperly denied. Alongside our partners who specialize in veterans' law, DAV helps the ill and injured veterans get the best possible representation at a time when it's vital to winning their claim.

Visit us at www. dav.org

The DAV service organization was the organization that had been appointed to represent my case. I had been notified several years ago that the DAV would represent me, however, they never contacted me.

I contacted the local DAV office in St. Petersburg, Florida with renewed hope. The brochure sounded convincing. The receptionists informed me there was no Representative available and she would ask one to return my call. A couple of days later the rep called me. I informed the DAV rep that I believed that I had proof the Veterans Administration was guilty of mishandling my case. As I tried to explain the evidence that I had discovered, the DAV rep stated that he had others calls to make and then the phone went dead.

This brochure was sent for the purpose of fund raising for their organization and not for the purpose of helping veterans.

It would be interesting to know the salary of their chief fund raiser.

Chapter Three: The System

Government Bureaucracy –   This was the beginning of a forty-year battle of denials and appeals followed with cover-ups, botched investigations, and a near death situations at the hands of the veteran's hospital in Tampa, Florida. Over four decades of disappointments, discouragement, and loss of respect for the Veterans Administration has ensued. In the meantime, the pain in my feet has increased every year since.

When I first filed a claim with the Veterans Administration I had no clue that forty-five years later it would still be unresolved. In my mind I felt that I had fulfilled an obligation to my country and my country had a moral obligation to me. I had a belief that all my injuries should be taken care of by the Veterans Administration. They quickly let me know they felt no obligation to me.

My first appeal had invoked a confidence because I believed I had provided enough information for them to locate my health records. They would confirm my claim. As usual the wait was a long time (it took over a year). Finally, another denial arrived. They stated once again that there were no records to be found.

Emotionally drained, it took several days to recover so a couple of weeks later I am still trying to figure out what to do next. During this recovery time another veteran, who had problems with the Veterans Administration, shared that a county veteran service officer in Bartow, Florida had helped him with a claim.

Chapter Three: The System

Mr. Ed Wright had been successful in assisting that veteran with the proper claim forms. It ultimately led to locating his health records. They had been lost at the Army Records center and his claim was later approved.

An appointment was scheduled to see Mr. Wright. At the appointed time Mr. Wright produced a copy of a ruling of the Board of Veterans Appeal (BVA) that was relevant to the disability claim for damaged feet.

The ruling was, ***Robinette V. Brown, App. 69-70 (1995) (Citing King V Brown 5Vet. App. 19, 21 (1993).***

It stated "Therefore, a lay statement from the veteran or another person about an incident in service, in this instance confirming a stressor for PTSD, is presumed to be credible for the purpose of establishing a well-grounded claim."

This was very exciting news. They had denied the claim because they said the health records could not be located, therefore, the claim could not be verified. This information gave me renewed hope. I felt that I could provide them with confirmation through "lay letters." As I left Mr. Wright's office I thought that I could now produce evidence that would support my claim.

After giving it some thought, I remembered a couple of military friends that would remember me being treated for a foot condition while I was stationed in Germany. However, it took some research. I discovered one lived in Henderson, Kentucky. This former friend's name was Bernie Bishop. I had met him in Germany and we became close friends. In those early years after returning to the states Bernie and I had kept close contact.

With very little difficulty Bernie was located. When asked if he remembered the feet problems and subsequent treatment that I had experienced while we were stationed in Germany, he readily admitted that he did. He also remembered the issuance of a "medical profile."

After explaining to Bernie, the "Lay letters" that were needed to support my claim, he was very willing to write a letter in support of it. The necessary VA forms on which the letter was to be written were sent to him. In a few days I received the signed letter.

Another friend, George Ray, had lived in Leitchfield, Kentucky. After several phone calls I discovered that George had passed away at a young age. He had developed a brain tumor and had since deceased.

Two of the of my relatives including my wife, wrote letters supporting the claim. The BVA ruling, **"Robinette V. Brown"** seemed to be the answer.

Mr. Ed Wright, the veterans service officer, assisted in submitting the letters to the Veterans Administration. Accompanying them was a request to re-open my claim since new evidence was presented.

Another claim denied – After another year, a notification letter was sent stating the request had been denied. The reason stated for denial seemed to be insane. They stated that some of the signatures on the 'Lay letters" were not legible and it resulted in the denial. The one they claimed that was not legible was the one from Bernie Bishop. In the letter he had enclosed his phone number and military service number. This information made the letter very easy to verify.

The denial of the request was appealed to the Board of Veterans Appeals in Washington, D.C. The following reasons were given asking the BVA to review the claim again.

<u>The lower appeals court did not consider the following:</u>

Robinetta V. Brown, 8 Vet. App. 69, 75-76 (1995) (Citing King V. Brown 5 Vet. App, 19, 21 (1993).

The reason stated by the Veterans Administration for not considering lay letters were as follows:

- Lay Letters had illegible authors.

  Fact: *The Lay Letter from a veteran provided not only a signature but also a phone number where the veteran could be reached. It also included his military service number. This person was stationed in Germany with the claimant. The other Lay Letters came from friends and relatives who had knowledge of this disability.*

  There were several things the lower hearing did not consider. The following is a list:

- *The fact that the United States Army was the custodian of all military records, including health records. It was their responsibility to make sure that all health records were preserved. They shifted complete and total burden of proof to the claimant.*

- *The lower hearing did not consider that the claim was first received in 1975, which put the claimant within ten years of his military service. It should have been considered as credible that the situation existed within a short time after serving in the military. Doctors verified that the situation had existed for years.*

- *The lower hearing did not consider the "buddy letters" that Board of Veterans Appeals had previously ruled in Robinetta V. Brown, 8 Vet, App, 69, 75-76 (1995) Citing King V. Brown 5 Vet, App 19-21 (1993).*

Contacting Senator Bill Nelson - Senator Bill Nelson (D Florida) was contacted and a request was sent requesting assistance in resolving this claim. Several months passed before Senator Nelson's office responded. The response letter actually came from the Veterans Administration addressed to Senator Bill Nelson and a copy sent to the claimant.

It stated:

"This is a response to your fax dated June 1, 2007, on behalf of Mr. Charles L. Pemberton.

Chapter Three: The System

"Status of receipt of submitted service medical records, "buddy statement," and Dr. Werd for evidence in appeal:
On October 4, 2004, Mr. Pemberton filed a Notice of Disagreement (NOD) based upon a VA decision dated August 19, 2004 denying service connection disability for bilateral flat feet, and ankle condition.
This decision stands without necessary documentation of condition stated while serving in the U. S. Army."

Senator Nelson sent a copy of this response letter and enclosed a note thanking the claimant for allowing him to help.

His reply seemed to say, "a fox had been hired to guard the hen house." It was believed by the veteran that Senator Nelson would use his influence to apply pressure on the Veterans Administration. They should have abided by the Board of Veterans Appeal's decision in **Robinetta V. Brown**.

It appeared this whole process was a political football game. They were just kicking the ball from one player to another. It is possible Senator Bill Nelson checked my political party affiliation and discovered that I was a member of a different political party.

A few days later, another letter from Senator Bill Nelson's office arrived. The following is an excerpt:

Aug. 9, 2007

Dear Senator Nelson:

In response to your inquiry requesting information on Charles L. Pemberton and his claim for disability for bilateral flat feet, and ankle problem. On April 7, 2005, Supplement of the Case (SOC) was released which confirmed and continued denial. On April 28, 2005, Mr. Pemberton filed a VA Form 9, Appeal to the Board of Veterans (BVA) and requested a Video Travel Board hearing. On August 4, 2007, his file was certified for shipment to BVA upon BVA's request.

A complete review of his file revealed six "buddy statements in support of his appeal, one statement from Mr. Pemberton, and medical documentation from Dr. Werd are on file.

On June 7, 2005, notification was sent to Mr. Pemberton that his service medical records were unattainable from the National Personnel Records Center (NPCR). The final response from NPCR was negative dated May 17, 1977. We have also requested medical records from his service department with the first attempt being April 19, 1976, second attempt being January 18, 1977, third attempt being May 7, 1977, and fourth attempt being July 11, 2005.

We have also approached Mr. Pemberton on June 7, 2005 and January 3, 2007, to provide copies of service medical records that he may have in his possession.

Chapter Three: The System

VA Request Records - The VA claimed they had requested my medical record at least four times over a twenty-eight-year period. They told me that I needed to hand over copies of health records that I had in my possession since they were unable to obtain medical records on me.

This was an absurd request since I was two weeks' shy of my 20th birthday when I received my separation notice from the military. What twenty-year old keeps any record for thirty days let alone thirty-five years.

Since the military was the custodian of all medical records and not the patient, most veterans do not see a need to safeguard their records.

Some health records were kept at the health care center where services were performed. Never had it been the responsibility of the veteran to provide a safeguard for their records. Could this be another indicator of negligence?

I continued my work as an educator because in that position I could do the job with minimal standing.

Appeal after appeal was filed with the Veterans Administration without any good news. Each appeal was denied locally and then it would be appealed to the Veterans Appeals Board in Washington, D.C. Denial after denial continued to arrive. The reason given on each one was that there was no proof that I was ever treated for a foot condition while I was in the military. Some appeals would take from three to five years.

As the years continued to pass, without finding a listening ear, hope once again faded. Whether it be the Veterans Administration or an organization whose specialty was helping the vet, there seemed to be very little hope of help.

Chapter Four: Lost Time

The continuing battle with the Veterans Administration - The Veterans Administration had notified me that the American Legion had assigned a representative to represent me with the Veterans Administration. It felt good receiving this news. I thought the representative should be contacting me soon. This never happened. There was no correspondence from anyone at the American Legion about the claim.

Another appeal was filed with a request for an in-person hearing at the local Veterans Administration, in St. Petersburg, Florida. Over a year later an in-person hearing was approved. Noticed was received of the date and time. Finally, I thought, I would be able to present my case with a person face-to-face. The rep from the American Legion was supposed to be present at the hearing. This certainly seemed like good news.

St. Petersburg, Florida is about two hours from my house. A couple of days was spent gathering information and any evidence that would help in the presentation.

The in-house hearing- A pre-conference meeting was set with a man at the Veterans Administration. Upon arriving, I checked in at the receptionist's desk. I was immediately advised that Mr. Smith (fictitious name, real name not remembered) was prepared to receive me. I was ushered into his office. This gentleman introduced himself and said that he was representing me in the in-person hearing. He was a rep with the American Legion. It felt good to finally meet the representative. However, immediately, suspicion appeared because the Veterans Administration was furnishing him a plush office within their facility.

He asked a couple questions and chatted about the great weather in Florida. He didn't appear to be prepared to represent my case. In a half hour I was ushered into a conference room. The American Legion representative followed and there were a couple other gentlemen inside the conference room ready to introduce themselves to me. One was there as a stenographer to video and audio tape the meeting. The other gentleman was the one to hear the case. The meeting was called to order and the narrator asked a few questions and I was given the chance to ask questions.

The meeting lasted about forty-five minutes and the American Legion representative did not ask one question or interject any thought.

When the meeting ended, it appeared that I had made a good presentation in support of my claim. They said that I would hear from them in the future.

Again, it was a long wait before I heard from the hearing officer. The wait lasted over a year. It was easy to think that the appeal had been lost, thrown away, shredded, or a dog ate it.

Finally, the verdict arrived. With much anxiety, I ripped open the envelope and again the letter stated that the appeal had been denied.

The reason for denial stated: "No new evidence was presented." At this time, the claim had been alive for about twenty-five years. My mind was going crazy. I begin to think they were delaying until they saw my name in the obituary or that I would give up appealing.

The filing of appeals continued, and they kept denying each one. Years were passing and the struggle with the Veterans Administration appeared to have no end. The claim remains alive and at the last count it had been over forty years since the first claim was filed.

After hearing stories from other veterans, it appears that this is a game that is played out repeatedly by the Veterans Administration. They acknowledge a backlog in claims and this acknowledgement has been going on for years.

The politicians keep promising if they get elected they will fix the problems with the Veterans Administration. After the election, nothing is ever done that improves the system.

Some claims seem to navigate the system very smoothly, however, about 50% of claims submitted are a never-ending nightmare. Many veterans become tired of fighting the system and simply drop out of the game.

Appeals Hearing and claim of treatment - Another appeals hearing was granted for December 21, 2005. Once again, an appeal of a denial had been submitted on the disability claim. The waiting game was being played out again. It took another year for a representative to contact me. With this notice I was advised that within a couple of days of the meeting that a Mr. John Newman would represent me. I thought that maybe this guy would hear me out and be a little sympathetic to my case. I was very anxious to meet him.

The day before the meeting he called and said that he wanted to have a meeting with me for thirty minutes before the hearing. I had no prior contact with him.

The next day, I located his office and like the other representative the Veterans Administration was providing him a plush office in their building. When the Veterans Administration is providing an independent representative with such benefits I could only ask, "was he really going to represent me?"

In the Appeals Hearing Rep. Newman stated, "Let the record note that it looks like Dr. Charles H. Vernick, on November 11, 1976, saw the claimant for treatment. The doctor gave an impression of bilateral plan valgus feet, and recommended the veteran have some arch supports made for his shoes to help his feet from overrunning his shoes."

Since I have limited knowledge in the medical field I consulted a medical dictionary to better understand the term "bilateral plan valgus feet." It defined it as: "An abnormally turned position of a part of the bone structure of a human being, especially of the leg."

Records of being treated by Dr. Vernick were requested from Mr. John Newman. His response was that the claimant would have to request them from the Veterans Administration. A request was sent twice to the Veterans Administration for these and any other medical records. Both times the request was ignored. This action violated their responsibility in assisting a veteran in obtaining records.

No further contact was ever established with the representative that had been assigned from the American Legion. A request for a different representative was later made. After a few weeks I was notified that a representative from the Disabled American Veterans Office had been assigned to represent me.

Below is a copy of a letter that was sent notifying him of the change.

TO: TRIAGE
RE: Mr. Charles Pemberton

Attached is VA Form 21-22. Please acknowledge appointment of the Disabled American Veterans as the above-named veteran's representative.

Thank you for your expeditious consideration of this request.
Sincerely

Gidget Rizzo
National Service Officer

This notification gave me hope that somehow the DAV would step up to the plate and persuade the Veterans Administration to stop playing games and look at my claim seriously.

Soon after they assigned a DAV representative they sent a second letter notifying me of a Travel Board Hearing. The letter stated that the meeting would be recorded, and a copy of the recording would be provided to the claimant. After the hearing, a request was made for a copy of the recording, however, they refused to comply.

It appeared that the bureaucracy and all its components treated veterans as uneducated, drug infested, homeless people. Men/women who had been called upon to give their all were now being treated as second-rate citizens.

Research revealed that there are literally thousands of veterans who are being disrespected, ignored, and left to die without any regard for their wellbeing.

America is currently surviving with an all-volunteer military. How would this work for American security if the message leaked out that veterans were being ambushed by the Veterans Administration. Today, young men and women leave their body parts scattered on foreign soil, believing the Veterans Administration has their back upon returning to the United States. What a rude awakening.

Another request for Health Records - After the fourth request was made to the Veterans Administration, they responded with twenty-seven —

year-old information. This sounded very much like no activity to find the health records had taken place in twenty-seven years.

The following was their response:

June 8, 2005

To: Charles L. Pemberton

Dear Mr. Pemberton:

In response to your request under the Privacy Act, the copies of your service medical records you requested are not present in your claims file. Several requests to obtain medical records were made. The final response was negative from the National Personnel Records Center dated May 17, 1977.

Sincerely

B.C. Gibbard
Veterans Service Center manager

Pain management was becoming less manageable by the month. Another appointment was made to see Dr. Matthew B. Werd, a Lakeland, Florida podiatrist. The first visit had gone well, and he gave this evaluation from the first visit.

Twice Ambushed

Dr. Werd stated:

April 12, 2005

<u>IOV</u>: This pleasant 59-year-old gentleman presented himself today complaining of continued problems especially with his right ankle. He states that this has been ongoing since 1964 although in the last five or six years his condition has actually worsened. He has seen several different physicians for his care.

He previously had a prescription orthotic, which he could not tolerate. Approximately four years ago, he had a foot fracture of the right ankle in two separate places, which required postoperative immobilization.

The patient did have increased swelling and effusion on the right ankle and the distal leg with hemosiderin deposits medially. Homans sign was negative bilateral. There was tenderness along the posterior tibial tendon. On weight-bearing, he had marked forefoot and midtarsal joint collapse and pronation.

X-Rays: The x-rays taken today are pending

DIAGNOSIS:

1. *Venous stasis right leg worse than left.*
2. *Degenerative joint disease of both feet*
3. *Marked adult acquired flat feet dysfunctional deformity.*

TREATMENT PLAN:

1. *Instructions on relative rest, ice, and elevation*
2. *Unna boot compression dressing right.*
3. *Follow up next visit to review x-rays and discuss further treatment options as needed. A prescription for Motrin 800 milligrams was dispensed. He might benefit from AFO Richie type brace if his condition has not improved. We might consider diagnostic ultrasound of the posterior tibial tendon on the right foot.*

Dr. Werd set a return appointment for me to return on May 9, 2005. The record for the March 9th visit stated:

"The patient returns today stating that he did have some relief from the Unna boot compression dressing. This had helped with the swelling, but he still has marked tenderness on palpation along posterior tibial tendon on the right foot and ankle.
X-RAYS: The x-rays taken last visit reviewed confirmed collapsing of the midtarsal joint with anterior break in the cyma line, decrease in the calcaneal inclination angle, as well as an incidental finding of a large posterior calcaneal enthesis."

DIAGNOSTIC: Posterior
Also I had a complete medical examination on my feet by Dr. Matthew Werd, The diagnosis was:
- *Venous stasis right leg worse than left.*

- *Degenerative joint disease on both feet.*
- *Marked adult acquired flat foot dysfunctional deformity.*

Dr. Werd said he could not determine at what age the joints of my feet had broken down only that it had happened after I had become an adult. Surgery was suggested as an option to consider. Dr. Werd said there was nothing further that he could do for treatment except surgery.

Armed with this additional information from a specialist, it was believed that the Veterans Administration would take another look at the claim. Actually, a verdict in my favor was expected. Instead, all medical records from the specialist were never considered. *The cover-up game continued to be played out.*

Another hearing was granted and scheduled for December 21, 2005. It took place at the Regional Office of Veterans Affairs at St. Petersburg, Florida.

The organizational representative that was assigned to assist in the claim did very little to assist.

Following is a copy of the transcript:

DRO: This is a hearing before **Michelle Aprile,** Decision Review Officer (DRO), sitting in at the United States Department of Veterans Affairs (VA) Regional Office at Saint Petersburg, Florida. In the case of **Charles L. Pemberton**, let the record reflect that the veteran has been sworn in, and he is represented by a representative of the Disable American Veterans Association (DAV). At this point, I will turn the hearing over to the DAV Rep., who will state the issues at hand and assist you in your presentation of your testimony.

REP: Thank you. The issues are services connection for an ankle problem, and new and material evidence adequate to reopen the claim for service connection for bilateral feet. Mr. Pemberton is here to present oral testimony in support of his claim for service connection for ankle and bilateral feet. We request that his testimony be accepted as new and material evidence in support of bilateral feet. At this time, Mr. Pemberton, you have a brief introduction that you'd like to give.

VET: Yes, I'm appealing the denial in a couple of areas here, in that the Board of Veterans Appeals in my opinion constitutes the equivalent of the Supreme Court and where procedures and precedent are established and; therefore, referrals made to the Board Decision of ***Robinette V. Veterans Administration*** states, "a lay statement from the veteran, or another person about an incident in service, in this instance, confirming his stressor for PTSD is presumed to be credible for the purpose of establishing a well ground claim." I submitted letters previously, and they were denied, because it says, in support of claim with illegible authors of lay statements and by a veteran who served with me in Germany does not constitute new and material evidence. In the case with **Robinette**, they ruled that the lay statements must be acceptable. The signatures may not have been legible; however, the body of the letter is. Service numbers and phone numbers were provided by each author where persons responsible for making decisions could have confirmed each signature with either a phone call or through the use of a computer. Those who did not serve with me still had knowledge of the conditions existing. The forms approved and supplied by the Veterans Administration requested an address and a phone number. The purpose for asking for a phone number is to contact the writer should there be any questions.

No such contact was ever made by the Veterans Administration to the writers of the letters. I believe the lay-letters, based upon the decision rendered in the **Robinette** case should have applied in my case.

Based upon that decision, the lay letters should be entered as new evidence in the original claim in 1976. This is new evidence that was not introduced at that time.

DRO: Right.

Vet: So, therefore, this would be in my opinion new evidence.

DRO: Let the record reflect that the copies are in your medical file.

REP: Okay, may I proceed?

DRO: You may.

REP: Okay, Mr. Pemberton, did you have flat feet when you enlisted into the army.

VET: No sir, or at least I wasn't aware of it. It was not determined on the enlistment physical. Had it been determined on the enlistment physical, they probably would not have accepted me into the service.

REP: When did you first notice your arches falling after you went into the service?

VET: I was in about two years. Severe pain in my feet began when I stood on them for long periods. At that point I went on "sick call."

REP: Okay, did they treat you while you were in the service?

VET: Yes, they did.

REP: Okay, where and how often, and what type of treatment did you receive?

VET: They treated me first at Benjamin Franklin Village Medical Dispensary in Mannheim, Germany. Basically, at that point, it was a visual, some x-rays, and they transferred me and the x-rays to the Military Hospital in Heidelberg, Germany. There they did further X-rays and issued a medical profile. The medical profile stated, "I could not wear combat boots, and that I was restricted to low quarters. A prescription was issued for low quarters to have special heels and the arches were built up with metal shanks. I was exempt from walking guard duty, no prolonged standing on my feet and I must sit down 15 minutes out of every hour.

DRO: Do you have both boots, by chance?

VET: No, I don't. This was 35 years ago.

DRO: Right

VET: It was a low quarter, it wasn't the boots.

DRO: Just trying to be helpful with any type evidence we have.

VET: Absolutely, I wish I did still have them.

REP: Okay, when was the first time that you were treated for the condition after you separated from the service?

VET: It was ongoing, I don't remember the first time I was treated.

REP: Okay, let the record note that it looks like Dr. Charles H. Vernick, on November 11, 1976, it appeared that he was seen then, and the doctor gave an impression of bilateral plan valgus feet, and recommended the veteran have some arch supports made for his shoes to help his feet from overrunning his shoes. Okay, are you currently being treated, Mr. Pemberton?

VET: Yes, I am.

REP: Okay, by whom, and how often.

VET: Dr. Matthew Werd, he is a foot and ankle specialist in Lakeland, Florida. I went through a series of treatment this past year that included a sonogram, and the prescription of a "Richie Brace."

REP: Now which foot?

VET: It's the right foot.

REP: Okay

VET: The right foot is more severe, and he (the podiatrist) determined that because of the way the ankles are turning, that the body weight had caused a sprain in the ankle. For five years, I have been walking on a sprained ankle. The podiatrist constructed a brace for my right foot to assist me.

REP: I'd like to introduce that as evidence. Have you ever had a doctor give an opinion as to whether or not your feet were aggravated by your military service?

VET: No

REP: Okay, why do you believe the VA should grant service connection for this?

VET: Well, because my condition was first discovered, and treatment was rendered while I was in service. I believe while serving in the U.S. Army, the duties affected the health of my feet.

REP: I have no further questions regarding this. Okay? Do you want me to proceed? Okay, let's talk about your ankle problem. Did you injure both of your ankles in service, or only one?

VET: I don't call it an injury.

REP: Okay

VET: It's a degenerate disc and this condition started while I was in service.

REP: So, you are having problems with both of your ankles.

VET: Both ankles

REP: And you believe your ankles were aggravated by bilateral feet?

VET: I'm not sure I understand; I know that you are calling it bilateral feet. In other words, flatfeet, but I don't think it's flatfeet. I think it is in the ankles because they are flipping over. The weakness in the ankle is allowing my feet to turn over. I don't know how to answer your question.

REP: Okay, so you wear a brace on your right foot?

VET: Yes, I do.

REP: And that supports your ankle?

VET: It is supposed to, but there is still a lot of pain.

REP: Okay, but what about the left ankle?

VET: The left ankle is in pain. I try to stay off them as much as possible. Throughout the last 35 years I've had to work jobs that did not require me to stand on my feet. Fact is, until two years ago I worked 19 years as a public-school teacher. During those 19 years, I could have sat down much of the time. In 2003 I was transferred to a different school and this assignment did not allow me to sit much. This forced me to apply for early retirement.
REP: Okay, are you taking any medications?

VET: I take Ibuprofen 800 mg. for pain.

REP: Okay, please tell us why you believe your current ankle conditions are related to your active duty?

VET: Because it goes back that far. It has progressively gotten worse over the years, but it extends back to 1964. Prior to that time, I never had any problems with my feet. And again, I believe had there been a problem they would have caught it on the enlistment physical. If the problem had existed prior to my enlistment and it had been discovered, then I would have been classified 4f (unfit for military duty). This was not the case.

REP: Let the record note that it appears that his record, his military records were destroyed in service. Taking that into consideration, that presumptive soundness that it's possible and probable that he had normal feet at the time he was enlisted.

VET: May I make a statement here?

DRO: By all means.

VET: The fact is that I first filed a claim in 1976. So, that should validate that there was a problem that far back. 1976 would have put me only 11 years away from the time I had served in the military.

REP: No further questions

DRO: Mr. Pemberton, this is your hearing. I want you to be sure that you've had an opportunity to say what you feel that you needed to state. Is there anything you would like to add before the hearing adjourns?

VET: I hope this is approved but if it isn't, it's been therapeutic for me. Having served during the Vietnam conflict, even though I was not assigned to a unit in Vietnam, I was assigned to Germany. Because of my age I had what I call non-combat PTSD (a teen-ager). I was subjected to a culture that did not support the American soldier. I was subjected to being spit on and rocks thrown at me. Being separated at Fort Hamilton, New York, we had to go through a debriefing where we were told to try and disguise ourselves when returning to civilian life. We were told it was for our good because the likelihood existed that we would not be treated very well as a returning veteran. While serving as a security guard in Seattle, Washington over 10,000 protestors marched down First Avenue where I was working at the Seattle First National Bank Building. I took this as a protest against me. Likewise, when the returning POW's plane landed on the tarmac there was no one to welcome them home, except their families. I believed them to be returning as heroes. I witnessed a private group attempting to raise monies to build a monument (Vietnam memorial) for the men and women who gave the ultimate sacrifice (their life). Many people even protested this project. It felt like someone having a birthday and having to give themselves their own party.

A few months later I received the official notice that the decision of the Bay Pines hearing did not go in my favor.

The next communication that I received came in the form of a letter from the local office of the Disabled American Veteran National Service Office.

Twice Ambushed

Contents of letter:

Dear Mr. Pemberton:

As your representative, this office has been advised by the Department of Veterans Affairs (VA) that you have been scheduled for a Travel Board hearing on October 17, 2007 at 8:30 AM (EST)

We recommend that you report to this office approximately one (1) hour prior to the scheduled hearing. This will allow time for us to discuss your case, review any new evidence, and ensure you fully understand the hearing process.

During the hearing, you will have an opportunity to offer testimony and evidence concerning your case. Additionally, you have the right to bring witnesses who may testify in your behalf. The Hearing may be recorded. If so, the testimony will be transcribed and you may be provided a copy.

If you are unable to attend, please notify this office as soon as possible.

Sincerely,

Katina Washington
National Service Officer

Chapter Six: Assistance Requested

By this time, discouragement and the feeling of being overwhelmed had engulfed me. Out of desperation I reached out to Senator Bill Nelson's office asking for help again. Senator Nelson is the Democratic Congressman from Florida.

The letter to the congressman reiterated the problem with the Veterans Administration. It is easy for the veteran to feel that he is the only one having problems with them. It was soon learned that the magnitude of the problem seemed insurmountable.

The feeling of isolation was acerbated at the local American Legion Post where I was a member. The Veterans Service Representative at the Post continually informed the members that all that was needed to be awarded benefits was to apply with proper documentation. He spoke of the Veterans Administration as a friend to the veteran.

The wait was on for a response from Senator Nelson's office. A lot of anxiety and suspense was generated during the wait. About a month later an official looking envelope arrived. With much anxiety, and built-up anticipation, I ripped open the envelope. Maybe this time, I thought that I would receive help from the senator. The envelope contained nothing but discouragement.

It read:

Twice Ambushed

Dear Mr. Pemberton:

In response to my inquiry on your behalf, I am enclosing a copy of the correspondence I received from the Department of Veterans Affairs, St. Petersburg Regional Office. I appreciate you giving me the opportunity to look into this issue.

If I can assist you with any other matter, please do not hesitate to let me know.

Sincerely

Bill Nelson

His response sounded so positive. The senator even "thanked" me for giving him an opportunity to help. There was a good feeling, after such a long time in this effort. I thought, finally, it seemed that someone was going to help. While waiting for the correspondence from the Veterans Administration, I stayed very positive.

A week later, another letter from Senator Bill Nelson's office arrived. Enclosed was a copy of the response from the Veterans Administration. What a let-down. I felt like someone had kicked me in the stomach. The air had been knocked out. This was not a new feeling. I had experienced this feeling many times since first filing my claim.

Chapter Six: Assistance Requested

Department of Veterans Affairs
Regional Office
P.O. Box 1437
St. Petersburg, Fl. 33731

May 3, 2007

Dear Senator Nelson:

This is in response to your fax letter dated April 13, 2007, on behalf of Mr. Charles L. Pemberton.
Status of appeal:
On April 7, 2007, a statement of the case (SOC) was released which denied service connection for: ankle problem, and bilateral flat feet. On April 28, 2005, Mr. Pemberton filed VA form 9, Appeal to the Board of Veterans Appeal (BVA) and requested a Travel Board Video Conference hearing. On October 24, 2006, a supplemental statement of the case (SSOC) was released which again denied service connection for: Ankle problem, and bilateral flat feet. Following the SSOC, there have been additional attempts to acquire evidence to support his appeal. Once a decision is rendered. Mr. Pemberton will receive notification detailing the reasons and basics of the decision If the appeal is not a full grant, his file will be forwarded to BVA for their review and decision.

Sincerely Yours,

Barry M. Barker

Twice Ambushed

After reading the letter from Senator Nelson I thought, "surely I am missing something." This was just a causal informative response to what appeared to be a causal request. There was nothing in this response that even suggested that Senator Nelson would actively pursue this matter.

The reply from the Veterans Administration to Senator Nelson's inquiry was filled with the usual run-around that they had been doing since the beginning of the claim. What was needed was a politician to stop being a politician and produce some results. Would that happen? The answer would come later.

Senator Nelson's office was asked to try again to help. He agreed to send another request to the Veterans Administration for documents regarding the claim. Several weeks went by and then another letter was received. It was a copy of their response letter to Senator Nelson's request. It stated:

Dear Senator Nelson:

This is in response to your letter dated May 10, 2007, on behalf of Mr. Charles L. Pemberton.

Status of Appeal

Mr. Pemberton initiated the VA appeals process by submitting a Notice of Disagreement on October 4, 2004, involving the following issues: Service connection for bilateral flat feet; and service connection for ankle condition. Mr. Pemberton formally appealed our decision by submitting VA Form 9, Appeal to the Board of Veterans' Appeals (BVA) videoconference hearing. It takes approximately 3 years from initial request to actual hearing date; therefore, we anticipate Mr. Pemberton will be scheduled on or after April 28, 2008. Should a vacancy become available sooner, we will immediately notify him of the date, time and place to report.

Service Medical records

We have made several unsuccessful attempts to locate Mr. Pemberton's service medical records (SMRs) over the past 30 years, and it is possible his SMRs were among 16-18 million federal records destroyed in a disastrous fire at National Personnel Records Center on July 12, 1973.

Because veterans often make a personal copy of their SMRs prior to discharge, we sent Mr. Pemberton a letter on January 3, 2007, asking him to submit copies of any personal SMRs in his possession. In our letter, we also informed Mr. Pemberton that we may be able to consider original or certified copies of any of the following substitute documents relating to his claimed issues: statements from military medical personnel; "buddy" statements or affidavits; state or local accident or police reports; employment or physical examinations; private medical evidence after military separation; letters written during service; photographs taken during service; pharmacy prescriptions; and insurance examinations. As of this date, however, we have not received a response.

False information - The above letter stated a couple items that were absolutely false.

(1) "Buddy" letters would be considered in place of health records. This consideration was never given to the claimant. "Buddy" letters were submitted along with private medical evidence and the claim was categorically denied. Absolutely no consideration was given to the "buddy" letters that were provided.

(2) It stated they had made several requests for the claimant's medical records from the National Records Center. A letter from the National Records Center was sent to the claimant that stated that the last time his health records were seen they were signed out by the Veterans Administration in St. Petersburg, Fl. They provided a code number that was used at the time it was signed out.

This was the first and last indication that any military health records existed on me during my tenure in the U.S. Army. A strong suspicion existed that the Veterans Administration in St. Petersburg, Florida had shredded the health records.

In this response, the tone of the letter put the burden of proof back on the claimant. They knew I did not possess any military health records. They were the custodian of medical records, not me.

Another appeal was sent to the Board of Veterans

Appeals in Washington, D.C. It was believed that they should accept the "buddy" statements in the absence of health records. After waiting two more years another reply was received.

This letter came from the Disabled American Veteran's National Service Office. The following is a copy of that letter.

Dear Mr. Pemberton

We received a copy of the recent decision by the Board of Veterans' Appeals (BVA) which remanded your case to the Appeals Management Center (AMC) U.S. department of Veterans Affairs Office (VA), located in Washington, D.C., for additional development. The BVA took this action to properly review your appeal: Whether new material evidence has been submitted sufficient to reopen a previously disallowed claim of entitlement to service connected for bilateral flat feet. Entitlement to service connection for a disability manifested by ankle problems.
Sincerely

Miguel A. Carrion

National Service Officer

Each letter such as this stirred new hope. It had been going on for so many years a little hope was better than no hope. The action of the Appeals Management Center remanded the claim back to the local Veterans Administration in St. Petersburg, Florida. The remand stated that the local VA had to take another look at the evidence provided.

It always takes a long time for the bureaucracy to respond. As usual, it was a long time in coming. Eventually it did arrive, and it was just another "denied" letter.

Senator Nelson's office continued to send copies of their correspondence from the Veterans Administration to me. Most of his requests for information seemed very generic. At this point I tried to stay positive. However, it appeared that the Senator was not getting very much done on my claim.

Senator Nelson's failure to persuade the Veterans Administration was again very discouraging. It was time for me to regroup my thoughts.

As I racked my brain to determine what direction I should pursue I remembered a former student that my wife had known when she was teaching at a local high school. He was now a U.S. Congressman from the State of Florida. What harm would it be to ask him to assist in this war with the Veterans Administration?

Chapter Seven: U.S. Congressman Putnam

Adam Putnam was the Congressman from the 12th District in the State of Florida. This is the district that I resided in. My wife had taught at the local high school where Congressman Putnam had attended earlier. I believed that since there had been some connection earlier he would put more effort into resolving the claim. A request for his assistance was sent to his office explaining the situation.

The first response from Congressman Putman's inquiry letter was received with encouragement. It was thought that with his help the Veterans Administration would take another look at my claim and resolve it favorably.

The following month Congressman Putnam requested records on my behalf from the Veterans Administration. Sometime later, a response letter indicated that they were sending a copy of my 201 personnel file. This file contains the veteran's military history. It does not contain any health records. Health records are contained in a separate file. The 201 files were useless in substantiating a claim.

Within a couple of weeks, a package arrived from Congressman Putnam's office with a letter that stated, "mission accomplished."

I revisited his office and informed his veterans service representative that I had received the wrong file. The representative advised that she would file another request for the health records.

A couple of months later a second copy of the 201

file arrived. Again, accompanied by a letter thanking me for allowing the congressman to help.

It seemed like the Congressman's service representative did not understand how to deal with the Veterans Administration. The VA had been hiding too many blunders and mistakes for a very long time. It would require a "get tough" action with the Veteran Administration.

Another year passes – I waited another year hoping that having Congressman Putnam as an ally a resolution to my claim was soon to come. It did not happen.

Communication with his office broke down and no communications transpired for many months. After a year or so another appointment was made for a consultation. It was discovered that a change had been made in the Congressman's office. The veterans' representative that I had dealt with before wasn't there anymore.

I was introduced to a young lady who did not know anything about my claim. When she tried to locate the file, there was none to be found. She said that she would have to start all over. My frustration level maxed out at this point.

I was back to square one. Years had gone by and I was very weary from dealing with the obvious. This was one of the times that I felt like giving up until I realized that was what they wanted me to do.

Realizing they wanted me to forget the claim would re-energize me to a whole new level. The young lady assured me that she would work to get this claim settled.

As usual, response time was slow. Weeks passed before I phoned the Congressman's office for an update. This phone call produced some activity and soon more letters arrived from Congressman Putnam's office. At least the Veterans Administration knew that I had not given up yet. They were to learn that I was going to be around for a while.

Each inquiry or appeal took very long for the Veterans Administration to respond. As the years passed there was no favorable action from them. They kept placing the burden of proof on me and this seemed so unfair. The custodian of records should have the evidence of a claim. Instead, they had made the records vanish.

Letters continued between Congressman Putnam's office and the Veterans Administration to no avail. It was always the same old same old. None of their responses brought anything new or any real encouragement.

Enclosed are copies of the correspondence that was received from Congressman Putnam's office.

Twice Ambushed

Congress of the United States
House of Representatives

Adam H. Putnam, 12th District, Florida

May 15, 2008

To: Mr. and Mrs. Charles L. Pemberton Sr.

Dear Mr. and Mrs. Pemberton

Thank you for your phone call to my district office concerning your problem with the Department of Veterans Affairs. I have forwarded an inquiry regarding obtaining your medical records to the Department of Veterans Affairs on your behalf.

I will contact you immediately upon receipt of any additional information regarding this matter. Meanwhile, if you have any questions or concerns, please contact my district office at 863-534-3530

Sincerely

Adam Putnam
Member of Congress

Congress of the United States
House of Representatives

Adam H. Putnam, 12th District, Florida

June 2, 2008

To: Mr. and Mrs. Charles L. Pemberton Sr.

Dear Mr. and Mrs. Pemberton

Enclosed is an interim response received from the Department of Veterans Affairs concerning your case.

I will contact you immediately upon receipt of any additional information regarding this matter. Meanwhile, if you have any questions or concerns, please contact my district office at 863-534-3530.

Sincerely

Adam H. Putnam

Member of Congress

<u>*Response to Congressman Putman's inquiry*</u>

A fax was sent to Congressman Adam Putman's office from St. Petersburg VA regional office in response to his inquiry:

Dear Congressman Putman
"We have received your inquiry. It is being given appropriate attention, and a complete reply will be made as soon as possible. Please refer to the control number shown above for any communication regarding this inquiry. Your interest and concern on behalf of your constituency is always appreciated.

Congressional Liaison
Varo St. Petersburg, Fl.

More Wasted time – Congressman Putman seemed to be my best hope, however, it turned out to be another couple of years of wasted time. After a couple of terms in Washington he retired from the congressional position and was elected Agriculture Commissioner for the State of Florida. Politicians keep changing positions while leaving the veteran behind.

One of Congressman Putnam's letters to the National Records Center invoked a response letter that absolutely was *chilling*. The following response letter was the first time that the agency admitted that my health records actually had existed. With their confirmation that the records had existed this was evidence that the Veterans Administration had in fact lied, delayed, and covered-up which had impeded the process.

This letter stated that my health records had been loaned to the Veterans Administration in St. Petersburg, Fl. It further stated that I could contact a Marlene Taylor for further assistance should I need it. I often wondered what information would have been gleaned if a call had been made to 314-801-0552. A note was included to ask for Marlene Taylor. Should she had given any information, the least that would probably happened, is that she would have been fired, if not completely silenced.

This information should be enough evidence to hold someone accountable for the extended delay of a claim.

However, when this information was submitted it did nothing to change the games the Veterans Administration was playing. This piece of evidence was ignored just like all the other that had been presented.

They continued to deny, delay and stall. Later it was discovered this was a national problem. It became apparent that the Veterans Administration was simply not going to cooperate.

Enclosed are copies of letters obtained from Congressman Putnam and the Military Records Center.

Congress of the United States
House of Representatives

Adam H. Putnam, 12th District, Florida

To: Mr. and Mrs. Charles L. Pemberton Sr.

Dear Mr. and Mrs. Pemberton

Enclosed is the response received from the National Records Center. I hope this information is helpful to you.

I appreciate the opportunity to have assisted you in this matter. If you have any questions or concerns, please contact my district office at 863-534-3530.

Sincerely

Adam H. Putnam

Member of Congress

National Personnel Records Center

Military Personnel Records
9700 Page Ave.
St. Louis, Mo. 63132

April 27, 2007

Honorable Adam Putman
Member, U.S. House of Representatives
650 E. Davidson St.
Bartow, Fl. 33830

RE: Veteran's name: Pemberton Charles
       Request Number 1-2895465207

Dear Mr. Putman:

The service medical records for the veteran have been lent to the Department of Veterans Affairs (VA). We suggest that you contact the nearest VA Regional Office to obtain copies of the records. You may call 1-800- 827-1000, under claim # 25672263

 If you have any questions or comments regarding this response, you can reach Marlene Taylor by phone at 314-801-0552.

Sincerely

R. L. Hindman

Director

Twice Ambushed

National Personnel Records Center
1 Archives Dr.
St. Louis, Mo. 63138-1002

Ref: Veterans Name: Pemberton, Charles
Request Number: 2-2049471480

Dear Recipient:

Thank you for contacting the National Personnel Records Center. The original medical record needed to answer your inquiry is not in our files; that medical record is with the Department of Veterans Affairs (VA). We suggest that you contact the nearest VA Regional Office to obtain copies of the records. If a claim has been filed with the VA it would be helpful to include the VA claim number when contacting them. You may call 1-800-827-1000 to locate a VA office near you.

If you have any questions or comments regarding this response, you may contact us at 314-801-0800 or by mail at the address shown in the letterhead.

Sincerely

Idella Jackson

Archives Technician

National Records Archives – This second confirmation came in May 2017. It was the second letter stating that the local Veterans Administration had been in possession of my health records.

The local Veterans Administration in St. Petersburg, Florida continued to deny that they had my health records in their possession. They have continued to deny possession of the health records from day one even after the National Records Center verified it was in their possession. *This sounds a lot like they are making records vanish.* The proper agency should be holding the Veterans Administration to a higher accountability. Not many government agencies can willfully make records disappear and not be accountable for their actions. The Veterans Administration can.

The National Personnel Records Center used the word *"deleted"* and "deleted copy" in one of their correspondence. It was a confusing choice of words. It sounded a lot like they are talking about disappearing records. The question is, did they intentionally delete my health records? Obviously, that is a possibility.

Notice the choice of words in the following letter.

Twice Ambushed

National Personnel Records Center
St. Louis, Missouri

Ref: Veteran's Name: Pemberton, Charles

Dear Mr. Putnam:

Thank you for contacting the National Personnel Records Center. We are pleased to respond to your request for Separation Documents and Personnel Records by providing the enclosed document(s).
Separation documents may include the following information: the type and character of discharge, authority and narrative reason for separation, reenlistment eligibility code, and separation program designator/number. If you are required a copy of the separation documents that does not contain this information, a *"**deleted**"* copy must be requested from the Center. A seal has been fixed to the separation document to attest to its authenticity.

Personal data pertaining to other individuals have been deleted from the enclosed documents.

Sincerely

R. L. Hindman
Director

Chapter Nine: Forty-Five Years Later

After forty-five years of claims, appeals and more appeals the battle with the Veterans Administration is still active. Today, I am limited to standing on my feet just a few minutes at a time. It seems all avenues relating to the claim have been exhausted. I am now seventy-three years old and it appears that my claim will never be settled within my lifetime.

It is obvious the Veterans Administration falls short of providing for the needs of many veterans. The VA has improved its services very little since the return of WW II veterans.

The incompetency in this organization is well known throughout government officials, however, all the veteran receives from them are empty promises.

The Veteran's hospital in Dayton, Ohio has seen many cases of incompetency according to the Dayton Daily News. In one such edition there was an expose' citing several veterans that had died because of slow care. At times, it took months for a veteran to be seen by a doctor.

"A Centerville man, whose Department of Veterans Affairs medical records were discovered in the attic of a former VA employee's home, has filed a federal lawsuit against the Dayton VA Medical Center alleging violation of his privacy as a patient, court records show.

The lawsuit alleged the VA didn't maintain security or have oversight procedures in place to prevent the removal of the files and that the federal agency was liable for the alleged "wrongful conduct" of the former employee."[1]

There is a ton of information on the internet detailing unbelievable incompetency within the system. The incompetency is not contained to one geographical area. It is happening at many of the veteran's facilities. There is no evidence that anything workable is being done to correct this blatant incompetency. In the meantime, the veterans and their families continue to suffer. Research information can be obtained from the internet by googling "Horror Stories in the Veterans Administration." One such research revealed the following stories:

Veterans, Families Share VA Healthcare Horror Stories, May 19, 2014.

"Steve Young, interim director of the Phoenix VA Health Care System, listened for hours last week to horror stories recounted by a crowd of hundreds of people. These people had lost or nearly lost, loved ones because of months-long wait times to see a VA doctor. Many of the patients had been "misdiagnosed and received poor treatment."

Dr. Samuel Foote, one of the whistleblowers who spent 24 years with the VA Health Care System, claims there are at least 13,000 patients without primary care doctors and many more who are unable to get prompt specialty or follow-up appointments.

The director of the Phoenix VA Health Care System and two others have been placed on administrative leave pending an investigation. The VA's chief health officer, Dr. Robert Pretzel, undersecretary for health in the Department of Veterans Affairs, resigned amid the confusion."

More out of the Phoenix VA Health Care System

"Darrell Richardson said his brother, Dennis, a Navy vet who served in Vietnam, was diagnosed in late July 2012 with liver cancer by his civilian doctor. When he went to the Phoenix VA hospital to seek treatment, he was informed it would take seven months to see an oncologist. They refused to even look at his records, he said. Dennis Richardson died four months later."

Lynn Morris' husband, Dennis Morris, continued to seek treatment even after turning 65, when he received Medicare, she said. In late summer 2013, Dennis Morris wasn't feeling well and tried for eight weeks to get an appointment at the Phoenix VA. He ended up going to the VA emergency room, where they did a chest x-ray and blood work and said he might have pneumonia.

They later took Dennis to a second VA medical clinic closer to home and they did a second x-ray and prescribed him antibiotics. When his condition did not improve, Lynn Morris took her husband to a civilian hospital. They immediately diagnosed him with stage IV lung cancer, and three weeks later he died. Mrs. Morris said she was convinced no one looked at the x-rays.

Twice Ambushed

Another story out of the Dayton, Ohio VA Health Care System.

"The Dayton Daily News has reported that the VA has admitted to 23 veteran deaths due to delayed care, but the newspaper said records it obtained through the Freedom of Information Act put the actual figure at about 1,100 between 2001 and 2013.

The VA makes more than 100 payments per year for claims that patients there died because of VA medical care, per the Daily News."

Memphis, Tennessee – A group of Memphis vets and their families met to share their horror stories after an investigation revealed errors by VA staff contributed to three deaths.

One veteran said, "that because they didn't act on the severity of my case, I had to have 18 inches of my intestine removed." He also stated that he went without food for three days.

Melvin Lesure arrived at the hospital swollen. Doctors told him and his fiancé Stephanie Davis, that it was the result of a cheese allergy.

A few days later he was dead. Hospital records showed he didn't have an allergy, he had MRSA.
"If they would have tested his blood work they would have seen he had MRSA," Davis said.

Now her family, like many others, wants answers. "We want to know what happened," she said, "why they didn't keep him? Why they didn't treat him?"

Chapter Nine: Forty-Five Years Later

Veteran Randy Weeks said, "We refuse absolutely to be mistreated by Veterans Administration or a VA hospital, so we are serving notice our voices will be heard."

Not much has been done to change the Veterans Administration over the last several years. Election after election comes and goes with politician after politician making promises and offering a glimmer of hope to the veteran. However, the Veteran Administration is just as messed up as it ever was.

What is it going to take to get results? Empty promises will never suffice. How long will our politicians and American citizens stand by and allow such incompetency in the Veterans Administration to continue? No veteran has ever been given recognition for giving their life at a VA Health Care facility.

The recognition comes from the battlefield where veterans acknowledge the potential of serious injury or sickness. It is very difficult for a veteran to mentally process the potential of becoming a casualty at a place (Veterans Administration) where they are supposed to be "friendly forces."

Lexington, Ky.- *A wife was told by doctors at the Veterans Hospital in Lexington, Kentucky that her husband had died. She questioned the doctor and was told they had done all they could for him. The wife asked if she could see her husband and after some persuasion he agreed to let her go to her husband's room. When she walked in she found that her* *husband's heart was still beating and in fact he was still alive. She decided to have him moved to a civilian hospital. He recovered and continued to live.*

"Some Veterans say Hospitals are in Shocking Shape"

Fourteen years ago, an ABC NEWS hidden-camera investigation ignited a firestorm about conditions and competence inside Veterans Administration hospitals.

Recently, there have been new stories of misdiagnosis, disastrous management, and deficient care at some of the nation's 162 facilities.

At a hospital near Cleveland, an ABCNEWS hidden-camera investigation found bathrooms filthy with what appeared to be human excrement. Supply cabinets were in disarray, with dirty linens from some patients mixed in with clean supplies or left in hallways on gurneys.

At a neighboring facility, examining tables had dried blood and medications still on them. In several areas, open bio-hazardous waste cans were spilling over. Primetime obtained internal memos documenting that the equipment used to sterilize surgical instruments had broken down — causing surgical delays and possible infection risk.

With 130,000 young American men and women putting their lives at risk in Iraq today, these conditions are particularly relevant. While current soldiers are treated at military hospitals, when they leave the service and need treatment, many will seek care at Veterans Affairs (as the Veterans Administration is now known) hospitals.

"Once you come back to be a veteran, it's like a black hole, you know nothing," former Army Sgt. Vanessa Turner told ABC NEWS.

Turner was stricken with a mysterious illness while on duty in Iraq this past year. She retired from the military on medical grounds, and when she reported to a VA hospital for treatment, doctors scheduled her for an appointment six months later." (It probably took that long to find any military health records or maybe they never found them).

Not a point of pride

Veterans who responded to a survey by the American Legion in 2003 said it took an average of seven months to get a first appointment at a VA hospital. In some hospitals, patients have waited as long as two years.

Jack Christensen – In 1999, Jack Christensen, a former army sergeant who served in the Korean War, was admitted to the VA hospital in Temple, Texas, with pneumonia, and ended up staying three years. Christensen's wife Pat, says the attitude of some of the practical nurses were shocking. Some of the patients were forced to beg for water and food, she says. Instead of helping her husband go to the bathroom, she said, "they will put a towel under his *hips and tell him to use the towel."*

She said her husband's condition worsened over several months. It became so bad that at one point he developed horrific bedsores and dangerous infections, and she says his doctors said they would have to amputate his legs.

His wife moved her husband to a private facility, where his infection healed, and he underwent extensive therapy. She sued the VA, and then used the money to pay for private care for her husband. The VA denied liability but paid a settlement.

There's also criticism of how the VA uses residents — doctors still training and not certified in their specialties. My cardiologists, who did his residency at the VA hospital told me that the VA hospital is good for training doctors but not good for patients.

VA hospital in Cleveland

Terry Soles served in the Navy during the Vietnam War. His wife, Denise, says he was a casualty of the Veterans Administration. In 1998, he went to the VA hospital in Cleveland, Ohio complaining of pain and diarrhea. The doctors removed small cancerous growths from his stomach and esophagus. The symptoms persisted over the next two years, his wife says the VA gave him painful tests and repeatedly lost the results. Per his wife, Soles was seen by a parade of constantly rotating resident doctors, and there was little consistency in his care.

Once, Soles was prepped for surgery but before the

operation the doctors, who were present, couldn't agree on what they were going to operate on, she said.

Before he got sick, the 6 foot Soles weighed more than 200 pounds. By the time his family finally decided to take him to a private hospital he weighed 80 pounds. Some VA doctors thought his problem was psychosomatic.

When he could no longer recognize his own son, Soles was rushed to a private hospital. There, Soles learned he was, "a total mass of cancer from his trachea to his renal bowel. There was nothing that could be done." Terry Soles died three days later. Dr. Jonathan Perlin, the deputy undersecretary for health said the Soles story was tragic, but added: "However, that is not the experience of most of the veterans who come to us for care."

Who is at Fault?

Critics charge that one of the big problems facing the VA is that too much money goes toward administration, at the cost of nursing and patient care. Dean Billik, the former director of the VA in Charleston, S.C., brought up an example.

In 1996, he was denounced for allegedly spending about $200,000.00 in taxpayer money to redecorate his office; $1.5 million to renovate a nursing home unit that stayed empty for two years; and tens of thousands of dollars for a fish tank in the lobby, while budget shortfall and staff cutbacks were contemplated.

Twice Ambushed

Congress heard testimony claiming Billik was "blatant in his mismanagement," and an inspector general's report confirmed several of the numerous allegations against him. After everything was brought to light, Billik still got a promotion. He was put in charge of the third-largest hospital system in the VA, encompassing eight cities, 295 acres of land and 83 buildings. His salary immediately jumped by $15,000.

Primetime obtained information on the central Texas VA system for Billik's six-year tenure at the top. It confirms that Billik cut spending $2 million for the people in direct patient care, nurses aides and practical nurses.

Other documents obtained by Primetime show that $129 million was spent on construction at three of six facilities in Temple, Texas. One source said $1.8 million was spent for renovating one building that was used for his offices, after it had been renovated for patient care.

Second Ambush - *The staging area for the second ambush is at the James A. Haley Veterans Hospital in Tampa, Florida and the Veterans Regional Office, St. Petersburg, Florida.*

In 2003, I retired from the Polk County School system after teaching in the system for twenty years. Upon retirement, I was only 58 years old. I was paying eight hundred dollars a month for health insurance. It was eating up a large portion of my retirement check.

After inquiring with the Veterans Hospital in Tampa,

Florida, I discovered that I was eligible for health care through the Veterans Administration. At this time, I applied and was accepted into their health care system.

All went well for a couple or three years, then a very serious mistake was made. Mistakes happen, the kicker was the way the system responded to the mistake.

Chapter Ten: Second Ambush

***A syncope (black out) while** driving* - In September 2009, I had a blackout while driving my truck on Hwy 640 near Hwy. 98 in Homeland, Florida. This is usually a high traffic highway since it is a connection between Hwy. 60 and Hwy. 98. Both highways are major highways in central Florida. After the blackout, my vehicle traveled about two miles while I was unconscious. The truck traveled over a railroad track, a river bridge and dodged oncoming traffic while travelling those two miles. When I regained consciousness, the truck was on the right shoulder of the road. At that time, I realized that my truck was off the highway and I swerved the truck to get back onto the highway. In swerving, I over reacted and two of the wheels left the ground and for several feet it traveled on two wheels. It came that close to turning over. After several feet, the two wheels came back down onto the highway, however, control of the truck had been lost. It finally came to rest in a ditch. I tried to drive it back onto the highway, but the truck was stuck. From out of nowhere came a car with several teenage boys and they stopped to help. They pulled the truck out of the ditch and when finished they disappeared as quickly as they had appeared. To this day, it is believed that there was divine intervention on my behalf.

A patient at the James A. Haley VA hospital – The next day, as I was thinking of the events, I became concerned as to the cause of passing out, so I called the emergency room nurse at James A. Haley Hospital. When I told her all that had happened she insisted that I come to the emergency room and be seen by a doctor.

Later that day, I was driven by my wife, to the James A. Haley Veterans Hospital in Tampa (sixty miles from my home). There I was seen by an ER doctor. A cardiologist was consulted, and a catheterization of the heart was ordered. In the cath lab, everything seemed to go as planned. After the procedure, I was placed back in my hospital room.

A couple of hours later, a trainee doctor from the college of medicine (South Florida University, which was next door) came to remove a plastic sheath that had been inserted in the groin area during the heart cath.

The doctor struggled in removing the sheath. It appeared he was having a problem. He left the room and reappeared about five minutes later. It looked as though he went and sought advice from someone who had more experience. He still had trouble removing the sheath, however, after another short struggle it was finally removed, and the doctor left the room.

The VA hospital is a training hospital for people entering the medical profession. It was understood that when a trainee doctor worked on a patient he was supervised by a more experienced doctor. There was no one else in the room except this trainee doctor.

Some of the Standard Operating Procedures were ignored and a more experienced cardiologist probably would have followed.

(1) After the heart cath they moved me back to my hospital room for recovery instead of placing me in a recovery room. In a recovery room my recovery could have been monitored by more experienced health care personnel.

(2) Pressure bandages should have been available and applied after the sheath was removed. They were not! This should have been a precaution in place in case of an emergency.

There were six patients in the room. Within a few minutes after the sheath was removed a cardiac care nurse (Caroline) came into the room to work on one of the other patients. Within a couple of minutes I felt like I was going to pass out. Just before I slipped into unconsciousness I shouted out to the cardiac care nurse that I was about to pass out. The last thing I heard was Caroline screaming for help. When I slipped into an unconscious state I could hear the voices of the health care workers, however, I was unable respond to them. Everything in my body had shut down except my hearing. Immediately, a call for assistance rang out and within seconds there were several health care workers taking care of me. One nurse lowered the end of my bed, so blood would flow to my head. Another nurse was shouting, *"we are losing him, we are losing him." A third nurse called out the blood pressure. It was 40 over 20.* I was unable to respond to any of their commands. One nurse was preparing me for a hit with the defibrillator.   Someone on the intercom was screaming, *"Code blue! Code blue!"* Soon, four nurses were running down a hallway pushing me on a bed at full speed. A nurse was riding on the bed with me. This nurse was holding an IV bottle with one hand while applying pressure to the heart cath incision with his other hand. They were transferring me to _the surgical intensive care unit._ While this emergency was taking place, there was no doctor in the room. The life and death situation were handled by several nurses. No doctor showed up until the next day according to the attending nurse.

Within the first week they called "Code Blue" on me three times. A hematoma that appeared on the left thigh swelled to thirty-two inches in diameter. The trainee cardiologist had created an aneurism.

I held on between life and death for the next fifteen days. While in Surgical ICU, a nurse said that a doctor told her to make sure I spent some time in a recliner. I informed the nurse that I could not make the move. She insisted that she had to follow the doctor's orders. Again, I said that I could not make the move from the bed to the recliner. She said she would assist in the changeover. The nurse was very small in stature and it was hard to believe that she could handle a man that is 6'2" and 250 pounds. She weighed about 120 pounds with two bricks in her pocket. She would be of little assistance should there be a problem. As I was leaving the bed to move into the recliner there was a tear in the incision area. That feeling of passing out swept over me again. I told the nurse that I was about to pass out and she said to go on to the recliner.

Immediately upon reaching the recliner I passed out. The nurse shouted for help and several people entered my room. Again, I was unable to respond to their commands. They asked if I could respond to certain things like move my toes or wiggle my fingers. I heard them speak but could not respond. It is uncertain as to how long I was unconscious.

Somewhere in the unconsciousness state, I heard someone who was saying, "Come on Charles, breath, come on breath, breath." Evidently, I had stopped breathing during that time.

For the next fifteen days, I remained in the James A. Haley Hospital as a patient. During the remainder of my stay they kept me in the Surgical Intensive Care Unit.

A surgeon came by a couple of times and said that he may have to perform surgery to close the artery that was punctured. A nurse discovered that the blood count was low. She said they would have to give me five units of blood and I was asked to sign a consent form.

When they administered the blood, the artery did not fix itself, therefore, the hematoma just grew larger and larger.

Children say the darnest things - One day, my seven-year-old granddaughter, Allee, came to visit me. While there, she laid her head on my chest and asked, "Papaw are you going to Heaven today?" I told her that I didn't think that I would be going today. She said,

Chapter Ten: Second Ambush

"If you go to Heaven today I want to go with you." That was a very emotional time.

A young female doctor came by my room most mornings to check on me. She seemed genuinely concerned. On one of her visits she said that she had never seen a hematoma that large. Each day the hematoma continued to grow as the blood in my body leaked out through the aneurysm that the doctor had created.

Doctors anxious to release him - On the fifteenth day a nurse said that the doctor had signed a discharge order. It seemed a bit premature since the aneurysm had not been fixed. After administering the five units of blood my blood count was up from 8 to 11, which was still low. It should be 13 or higher. They just assumed that the leak had been fixed. My body told me that I was not out of the woods yet. I expressed concern to the nurse and she said she had no choice since the doctor had signed a release paper.

While there as a patient, the nurses who took care of me were very "hush hush" about my condition. When questions were asked, they were very evasive. One male nurse (a registered nurse) even asked if a lawsuit was going to be filed (This was not my intentions at the time, I just wanted to get well). The nurse became very chatty after he was told that no law suit was in the makings. He said there had been some mistakes made and if he was in my shoes he would consult an attorney. He told me that if what he had said was repeated to anyone that he would deny saying it.

One day a friend called, who happened to be a nurse. She had worked in the medical field for several years. During the conversation, I told her about how the nurses were acting strange. She volunteered to visit and talk with the nurses since she knew their jargon. Later she arrived and spoke to some of the nurses. Upon leaving she said that something strange was going on.

The doctors seemed very anxious to release me from the hospital. My condition had not improved to the level of being released. The same male nurse, who had talked with me earlier, came into my room the morning of my release. He said that he thought they were making a mistake releasing me from the hospital so soon. He made it very clear that if a lawsuit was going to happen then he didn't want to discuss anything with me.

When I complained to the nurses that I felt that I was too sick to leave the hospital, they assured me that I didn't have a choice. It was always the same response, "The doctor has signed the release form, so you have to go home." The minimum care at this point should have been to verify that the artery had stopped bleeding. This did not happen. It could have been verified by a simple blood test.

Upon arriving home, I felt very sick. The second day I was so sick that I realized that I needed to go back to the hospital. My wife drove me to the emergency room at Bartow Memorial Hospital.

Chapter Ten: Second Ambush

The two days that I had been home, it had been an almost impossible task to get from the bed in the bedroom, to a recliner, in the family room. I could not do anything other than sleep all day. When I called the VA Hospital, a nurse assured me that it was a normal recovery. She said that my body had been beat up badly while I was in the hospital. She further stated, "with what your body had been through the recovery was going to be more difficult."

Two days after leaving the James A. Haley Veterans Hospital I found myself in the Emergency room at Bartow Regional Hospital. I felt that I was at the point of death.

Upon arriving at the emergency room, I explained to the nurse in triage what I had gone through at the VA hospital. Looking at the hematoma the nurse quickly noted that I needed to see a doctor STAT.

The admitting nurse asked me if I had ever been seen by a doctor at that hospital before. I told her that I had been a patient there the year before (2009). The attending physician at that time was a Dr. Feliciano. On that visit I was diagnosed with an irregular heartbeat. The condition was treated with a blood thinner called "heparin." They again assigned Dr. Feliciano as my primary physician.

This visit was in 2010. After conducting tests, they discovered the artery was still leaking. The blood count was low. They admitted me to Intensive Care. I would need five more units of blood. It had only been a week since I had been given five units of blood at the James A. Haley Hospital. Within two days, here they were giving me another five units of blood which meant I had received ten units within a week.

The policy at the Veterans Administration is that they will pay the bill only till the patient is stabilized. A social worker was immediately assigned to my case. She requested for me to be transferred back to the James A. Haley Hospital in Tampa, Florida.

The social worker assured me that she had been in touch with the social worker at hospital in Tampa. Later that evening the social worker returned and said that the VA had responded to her request. Their response was that they did not have a bed available. The next day I was told by the social worker that she had submitted a second request for a transfer. The VA responded with, "they would not receive a patient from the Intensive Care Unit." They stated that any patient in the Intensive Unit was too sick to be moved.

It was requested that a surgeon see me. The next day, Dr. Miller, a Winter Haven surgeon, stopped by and examined my hematoma. He said that surgery was necessary to vacuum the blood out of my leg. It was scheduled for a couple days later.

As the blood continued to seep into the hematoma the pain became unbearable. I requested medication from the duty nurse to assist in the pain management. The nurse said that the primary care physician refused to prescribe anything for the pain. The pain was going to a level that I could hardly bear. The nurse further stated that the primary care physician said that the pain was just in my head. At that point I felt like I wanted to give him some pain.

With some persuasion from me, the nurse contacted Dr. Miller, the surgeon, and he gave the approval for an injection to be administered. That evening after receiving the shot the pain subsided. Soon, I drifted off in a sleep that seemed like heaven. I had no sleep in the last three days.

On the fourth day, Dr. Miller, stopped by to check in on me. He said the thigh surgery had been scheduled for the next day.

During surgery over 500 cc's of blood were vacuumed from the hematoma. Prior to the surgery, another attempt had been made for my transfer back to the James A. Haley Veterans Hospital. All attempts failed. Each attempt was followed by a different excuse.

More attempts made to transfer - For seven days, the social worker at Bartow Regional Hospital worked with the patient advocate at James A. Haley Hospital in Tampa to have me transferred back to that hospital. Since this medical condition was created at the James A. Haley Hospital she thought it would be an easy task to have a transfer approved. This proved to be an impossible task. A transfer approval was never granted.

The powers that were making the decisions at the Veterans Hospital continued to meet the requests for transfer with excuses. One day it was "no beds available." Another day the excuse was "they could not accept a patient from the Intensive Care Unit." Another excuse was that "the patient was too sick to be moved." The last one was "they didn't want to obligate themselves for the cost of transporting." They created this life-threatening issue so what was the problem?

The social worker continued to work tirelessly with

the Veterans Administration to acquire approval for my transfer. Every day she would return to my room and give me an update on her progress with the VA hospital. Every time they would come up with an excuse to block my return to the VA hospital.

I was dismissed seven days after being admitted to Bartow Regional Hospital. Upon being released a follow-up appointment was scheduled with Dr. Miller. The follow-up appointment was to have surgical staples removed. He charged me a fee of one-hundred dollars for their removal. It seemed a little strange for this particular charge since it was a post-surgical procedure. I asked the doctor, why the charge? I thought the fee should have been included in the cost of surgery. Dr. Miller said that he would not receive any money from the Veterans Administration for doing my surgery and the hundred dollars would be all that he would receive. It was hard to believe that the Veterans Administration would treat one of their own this way.

I was sent home to recover and it took a year to get back to where I was before the experience at the Veterans Hospital. *The original aneurysm created at James A. Haley Veterans Hospital became a secondary issue. The primary issue at hand was my recovery.*

My wife, Mary, and I were administrators at a Faith-based private school. For that recovery year, I was of little use to the school. There was a reclining chair in one of the private rooms and that is where I spent most of my time during the day. I had always been an active person and it reduced me to a shell.

Boredom sets in - After a few weeks of recovering, boredom set in. At times I needed something to entertain myself. I chose to pull a few pranks on the students. They provided the audience I needed for my entertainment. On one such day an opportunity availed itself that I could not pass up. It was one of those days that I had slept for several hours in the recliner. Mary asked some of the students to go into the room and wake me. As they entered the room I pretended to be asleep. They asked me several times to get up and I continued to pretend to be asleep. One of the girls came over and shook me trying to get me awake. After a few minutes, they left the room. They could be heard saying to Mary, "he won't wake up, he may be dead." Mary told them to go back into the room and try one more time to wake me up. This was becoming fun. I continued to pretend until they were near my recliner. As they approached I lunged at them with a loud shout. Boy, did that scare those girls.

It can't be proven, but they may have thought the thing that happened to Lazarus, in the Bible, had just happened again. Those girls were terrified. From that day forth it was difficult to entertain myself at their expense.

The VA hospital continued to refuse to accept responsibility for the life-threatening situation they had caused me.

After a few months of recovering I felt that I wanted to know what had gone wrong at the veteran's hospital. This procedure was such a common one. I requested a copy of my health records that covered the fifteen days that I had been a patient in their hospital.

After filing a written request with the hospital and waiting several weeks I finally received over five-hundred pages of documents. Hours were spent going through the documents and there were no indication of the problem they had treated me for. Finally, I gave up. There was only a casual mention of a hematoma or the fact that I had received five units of blood. Again, it was an excellent job of burying the real cause and treatment.

A few weeks later, I received a veteran's brochure that provided information on how to file a claim for compensation. The brochure listed five reasons for filing a claim. One reason given was for "error in judgment." The VA doctors had errored in judgment by discharging me before the hematoma had stopped bleeding. The hematoma had created a life-threatening situation, this was serious stuff. They knew they had messed up, so it was time to cover their tracks.

A claim for compensation based on "error in judgment" was filed and the first response to the claim was denial. This began another series of appeals and denials. It was reminisced of the old days when claims were filed and was followed by a denial then an appeal and then a denial.

A claim filed - When the claim for "error in judgment" was filed, certain information that was used to deny the claim was fraudulent. The claim stated the patient was released prematurely which created an "error in judgement."

The Veterans Administration's investigator claimed that I had been a patient at Bartow Regional for an irregular heartbeat. It said evidence showed that I was treated with "Heparin" and this was the cause for the hematoma.

The investigator focused on a 2009 stay in the hospital when I was treated for an irregular heartbeat. This incident happened a year before being a patient for a hematoma. Trickery was being used again to deny a claim. Wrong information gathered by the Administration's investigation was used once again to deny my claim.

The greatest obstacle to overcome is the feeling of abandonment and not knowing who to turn to for help. This feeling is almost over powering and I was getting hit hard by it.

I felt like a boxer going a few rounds with the heavy weight champion of the world, being beat up badly in round one and now it was time to go for round two.

Chapter Twelve: The Battle Rages

I was still bruised from my thirty-five-year battle with the Veterans Administration on a claim for a service connected disability. It was going to be difficult enduring another bout. However, the more I thought about the way the Veterans Administration treats veterans, I could not turn it loose.

I thought that the Veterans Administration was going to get away with almost killing me. After the blunder they just brushed it off as nothing. They could not get away with that or, so I thought.

Once again, I sought the aid of my Congressman and Senator. The Veterans Administration's culpability of incidents had been showing up regularly on the six o'clock news. I thought maybe they would react differently since their blunders were making the news.

An appointment was set-up with the Congressman's aide, who handled the veteran's affairs. I believed this meeting would produce positive results. Congressman Putnam's aide was about twenty years old. Upon meeting her I wondered if she knew anything about the Veterans Administration.

I explained my situation and asked if Congressman Putnam would assist in resolving my disability claim. She assured me that he would do everything he could. I left the congressman's office thinking there would be a positive resolution.

Another letter arrived from the Veterans Appeals Board. They continue to refuse to accept the fact that the hospital made a serious blunder in the medical treatment of a patient. I would not have pursued the claim so aggressively had they accepted responsibility for their mistake and tried to rectify it.

In a conversation with a cardiologist who was trained at James A. Haley Hospital, I explained to him the problems I had encountered. The cardiologist remarked, "it sure sounds like some mistakes were made."

Human error is possible - When humans are involved mistakes can happen. However, when a mistake is made it should be rectified as soon as possible. Most of the medical staff at James A. Haley Hospital do an incredible job. It is when the bureaucracy gets involved, then mistakes are purposely gone unfixed. It is the top management that must have a complete overhaul. The bureaucrats must be held accountable. Research shows the bureaucracy at the Veterans Administration to be complacent and they show little concerned for our veterans. Too many good men and women are subjected to unbelievable experiences at the hands of the ones appointed to take care of them.

Workers in-charge at rest homes, hospitals or any other facility outside of the Veterans Administration would be put in jail if they treated their patients the way the Veterans Administration treats many of their patients.

There are many great doctors and staff workers who work in these facilities. It is not the intention of this expose to castigate every one of them. The medical staff at the local facility cannot fix the system.
Yet, oftentimes, they are the ones who take the heat.

Chapter Twelve: The Battle Rages

They take the heat because the upper management is good at passing the buck. Research shows that the upper management are the ones who stall, lose records, destroy records, and generally play the "wait game." Remember the "wait game?" This is the one where they hope the veteran will die before resolving his/her issues.

Letters continued to flow between the Veterans Administration and me. On an occasion, a letter would arrive from a Senator or a Congressman.

It was discovered that the Veterans Administration has trained the politicians to play their game and the politicians continue to fall prey to the monster.

For over forty years there was hope and then it would be crushed. This would happen over and over again. Now it appeared that the Veterans Administration was impregnable. Forty years ago, it was unimaginable that a veteran would have to deal with the Veterans Administration so long to resolve an issue.

Enclosed is a copy of one of the incoming letters:

Twice Ambushed

Department of Veterans Affairs
Board of Veterans" Appeals
Washington, D. C. 20038

To: Charles L. Pemberton

Dear Mr. Pemberton:

We have completed the steps directed by the Board of Veterans' Appeals when they remanded your appeal. We are returning your VA records to the Board in Washington, D.C. The board will notify you when they receive your records.

If you want to send the Board additional evidence concerning your appeal, submit a new request to appear personally before the Board to present testimony, or appoint a representative or change your representative, you must explain to the Board in writing why you could not send your request or accept your new evidence. Any such new evidence or request, together with your explanation of why these items could not be submitted earlier, should be sent to: Board of Veterans' Appeals (OIE), 810 Vermont Ave. N.W. Washington, D.C. 20420.   Be sure to include the Veteran's name and VA claim number in your letter. If you are not a veteran, also include your own name. Do not send such material to this office.

If you have any questions about the time limit for

submitting new evidence, appointing or changing a representative, or asking for a hearing before the board, please consult your representative or see 38 C.F.R. &20.1304.

The Board will notify you in writing as soon as it has made a decision in your case.

Thank you for your service,

RO Director
VA Regional Office
Cc: DAV

Another letter for the files, however, it brought very little hope. To think that a system, such as our nation's agency for taking care of their military can be in such a disgraceful shape. It is unthinkable!

Twice Ambushed

Sept. 21, 2016

Ref: Charles L. Pemberton

Dear Appellant:

The Board of Veterans' Appeals has made a decision in this case, and a copy is enclosed. The records are being returned to the Department of Veterans Affairs office having jurisdiction over this matter.

The Board of Veterans Appeals has partnered with J.D. Power and Associates to determine how our customers perceive the service we provide as an organization. You may be contacted by telephone from someone at J.D. Power and Associates in the next 30-60 days and asked to provide feedback on your experience with the Board of Veterans Appeals by taking a brief survey. We appreciate your willingness to help us improve our processes and the service we provide for Veterans by participating in this survey. Any comments provided to J.D. Powers are 100% anonymous and will not impact the delivery or timing of any future benefits provided by VA.

Thank you in advance for your willingness to participate and share your feedback.

Sincerely yours,

John Z. Jones

Interim Director, Office of Management, Planning and Analysis

Enclosure:

The Tampa VAMC (Veterans Administration Medical Center) has not responded to the Veteran's notice of disagreement, to include issuing a statement of the case regarding this issue. Under those circumstances, the Board is obliged to remand this issue to the AOJ for the issuance of a statement of the case. Stegall V. West, 11 Vet. App. 268 (1998); Manlincon V. West, 12 Vet. App. 238, 240-41 (1999)

According, this case is REMANDED for the following action:

1. *The AOJ must take appropriate action and issue a statement of the case that addresses the issue of entitlement to payment or reimbursement of unauthorized medical expenses. The Veteran should be informed that, in order to perfect an appeal of this to the Board, he must file a timely and adequate substantive appeal following the issuance of the statement of the case. This issue need not be returned to the Board unless Appellate review is otherwise perfected.*

The Veteran has the right to submit additional evidence and argument on the matter the Board has remanded. Kutscherousky V. West, 12 Vet. App. 369

(1999).

The claim must be afforded expeditious treatment. The law requires that all claims that are remanded by the Board or the United States Court of Appeals for Veterans Claims for additional development or other appropriate action must be handled in an expeditious manner.

Thomas J. Dannaher

Veterans Law Judge, Board of Veteran's Appeals

The letters from the Veterans Administration kept coming.

Listed below are some of the most recent letters from the Veterans Administration.

**Department of Veterans Affairs
Board of Veterans' Appeals
Washington, D. C. 20038**

Sep. 21, 2016

Ref: Charles L. Pemberton

Dear Appellant:

The veteran served on active duty from July 1962 to June 1965.

This matter comes before the Board of Veterans Appeals (Board) on appeal from an April 2010 rating decision of the VAMC in Tampa, Florida, which denied entitlement to payment or reimbursement of unauthorized medical expenses resulting from private hospitalization in September and October 2009.

In March 2015, the Board remanded the claim for further development. For the reasons discussed below, the Board finds that there has been substantial compliance with the development sought as part of the March 2015 remand. Stegall V. West, 11 Vet. App. 268 (1998). Veterans Benefits Management System (VBMS)

Twice Ambushed

This appeal was processed using virtual VA and the *paperless claims processing system. Accordingly, any future consideration of this case should take into consideration the existence of this electronic record.*

The appeal is REMANDED to the agency of Original Jurisdiction (AOJ). VA will notify the veteran if further action is required.

Remand

In an April 2010, administrative decision, the Tampa VA Medical Center considered and denied payment or reimbursement of the unauthorized medical expense incurred by the Veteran as a result of private hospitalization at the Bartow Regional Medical Center in September and October 2009 for post-surgical treatment of a hematoma.

In May 2010 written statement to his accredited representative, which was later forwarded by that representative to VA, the veteran expressed disagreement with the April 2010 determination. The Board finds this written statement, specifically referencing the April 2010 denial and subsequently forwarded to VA by the representative, to constitute a notice of disagreement regarding the denial of payment or reimbursement of unauthorized medical expenses.

The Tampa VAMC has not responded to the Veteran's notice of disagreement, to include issuing a statement of the case regarding this issue. Under these circumstances, the Board is obligated to remand this issue to the AOJ for issuance of a statement of the case, *Stegall V. West, 11 Vet. App. 268 (1998); Manlincon V. West, 12 Vet. App. 238, 240-41 (1999).*

Sincerely Yours

John Z. Jones
Interim Director, Office of Management
Planning and Analysis

As of now, the claim is still being debated by the Veteran's Appeals Board in Washington, D. C. The last letter received was in July 2017. I believe there is no end to a claim being considered by the Veterans Administration. I am now seventy-three years old and the claim was first initiated when I was about twenty-eight years old. It is still in the appeals process.

There is amazing evidence that the Veterans Administration does stall, in hopes the claimant will die. This is the way they resolve many of the veteran's claims.

Twice Ambushed

Department of Veterans Affairs Regional Office

"Supplemental Statement of the Case"

June 08, 2017

Decision:

Entitlement to compensation benefits for residuals of cardiac catheterization surgery, to include a punctured artery, pursuant to 38 U.S. C.A. 1151 is denied.

Reasons and Rebuttals:

This supplemental statement of the case is made pursuant to the Board of Veterans' Appeals Decision dated September 21, 2016, Docket No. 12-21 391.

Board of Veterans' Decision dated September 21, 2016, Docket No. 12-21 391 together with all evidence identified therein, remanded the issue of entitlement to compensation benefits for residuals of catheterization surgery, to include a punctured artery, pursuant to 38 U.S.C.A. 1151 pending additional development. Based on review of the available evidence, we have made the following decision.

VA medical opinion from VISN 8 Regional Office dated March 24, 2017 provided an opinion that (1), the claimed failure to timely diagnose and properly treat the hematoma that arose from a punctured artery during the cardiac catheterization surgery was less likely than not (less than 50 percent) to have occurred; (2), the claim disability was less likely than not (less than 50 percent) caused by, or as a result of carelessness, negligence, lack of skill, or similar incidence of fault on the part of the VA personnel; (3), the additional disability of the residuals of the cardiac catheterization surgery to include a punctured artery was at least as likely as not (50 percent or greater probability) caused by, as a result of an event that could have reasonably been foreseen by a reasonable healthcare provider; and (4), the assertion of active internal bleeding at the time of discharge and that further treatment or testing should have been performed prior to discharge was less likely than not (less than 50 percent) to have occurred.

The examiner did indicate that VA medical records did demonstrate by the treatment that an artery had been punctured. Diagnostic testing and, a subspecialty input was in place in order to address the issue during the time of September 2009 hospitalization at the Tampa VA facility. This particular problem was one that could arise due to any surgical procedure of this type.

The veteran is aware that this problem could arise during any surgical procedure. However, the medical personnel were not expecting any problem to arise. If they had expected a problem then they would have been prepared for it, which they were not. It was an unintentional and often unavoidable part of the operation. The fact that it occurred reflected the *nature of the procedure rather than due to carelessness, negligence, lack of skill, or similar incidence of fault on the part of the attending VA personnel. As such, the standard for medical care was such that the healthcare team monitors an individual for potential issues and then works to address any problems that may arise. The chart notes that this did occur. In addition, VA notes demonstrates treatment and evaluation on several occasions for hematoma while hospitalized. This included imaging studies and serial Hemoglobin determinations in order to determine if there was active bleeding.*

Compensation is payable for any disability which is caused by VA hospitalization, medical or surgical treatment, vocational rehabilitation, compensated work therapy program (CWT), or as the result of having submitted to a VA examination. The evidence must show that the veterans' disability is actually the result of the VA care. Specifically, carelessness, negligence, lack of proper skill, error in judgment, or similar instances of fault on the part of the Department in furnishing the hospital care, medical or surgical treatment.

Rebuttal by the veteran

(1) For the VA to render a verdict of denial on this claim they had to ignore, destroy, alter records, and absolutely deny what was very evident. The admittance to Bartow Memorial Hospital two days later and the veteran being given five more

units of blood was confirmation that bleeding was still taking place. A surgeon having to do surgery and remove over 500 cc's of blood from a thirty-three inch hematoma should have been enough evidence to confirm the claim.

(2) I asserted on numerous occasions, after the cardiac catheterization, and prior to being dismissed, that the hematoma was still leaking blood. Two days before being dismissed from James A. Haley VA Hospital five units of blood was administered to me.

(3) I was not placed in a recovery room for the removal of a plastic sheath placed in the incision during surgery. By not being in a recovery room, the doctor was not equipped to handle a mishap. Pressure bandages and the likes were not available.

(4) A Healthcare provider, with any experience, could have foreseen the possibilities of something going wrong. Experience would have told him to be prepared for something to go wrong, which he was not.

(5) It would have been easy to ascertain that internal bleeding was still active since I was given five units of blood two days prior to being dismissed from the hospital.

They continue to deny that mistakes are made at the VA hospital.

Twice Ambushed

The responses from the Veterans Administration continued to sound like a lot of double-talk and jargon that could be interrupted in many different ways.

From day one the Veterans Administration had determined that this claim was going to lose in the Court of Appeals. Regardless of the evidence that I provided it was going to be ignored.

Many veterans who have not experienced dealings with the Veterans Administration will shake their head in disbelief. That is because this whole nightmare is unbelievable. However, many veterans will relate and feel relief that they are not the only ones experiencing such a nightmare.

In the early stages of gathering material for this manuscript it would have been hard to comprehend the scope of such incompetence.

Chapter Thirteen: Run-Around Continues

**Board of Veterans' Appeals
Department of Veterans Affairs
Washington D.C. 20420**

In the Appeal of Charles L. Pemberton:

Docket No. 12-21-391

*On Appeal from the Department of Veterans Affairs
Medical Center (MC) in Tampa, Florida*

The Issue

Entitlement to payment or reimbursement of unauthorized medical expenses resulting from private hospitalization in September and October 2009.

(A separate decision will be issued on the issue of entitlement to compensation benefits for residuals of cardiac catheterization surgery, to include a punctured artery, pursuant to 38 U.S. C.A. 1151)

Representation

Appellant represented by: Disabled American Veterans

Attorney for the Board

C.S. DeLeo, Associate Counsel

Twice Ambushed

Introduction

The Veteran served on active duty from July 1962 to June 1965.

This matter comes before the Board of Veterans Appeals of appeal from an April 2010 rating decision of the VAMC in Tampa, Florida, which denied entitlement to payment or reimbursement of unauthorized medical expenses resulting from private hospitalization in September and October 2009.

In March 2015, the Board remanded the claim for further development. For the reasons discussed below, the Board finds that there has not been substantial compliance with the development sought as part of the March 2015 remand. Stegall V. West, 11 Vet. App. 268 (1998).

This appeal is REMANDED to the Agency of Original Jurisdiction (AOJ). VA will notify the veteran if further action is required.

Remand

In an April 2010 administration decision, the Tampa VA Medical Center considered and denied payment or reimbursement of the unauthorized medical expenses incurred by the veteran as a result of his private hospitalization at the Bartow Regional Medical Center in September and October 2009 for post-surgical treatment of a hematoma.

In a May 2010 written statement to his accredited representative, which was later forwarded by that representative to VA. The veteran expressed disagreement with the April 2010 determination. The Board finds this written statement, specifically referencing the April 2010 denial and subsequently forwarded to VA by the representative, to constitute a notice of disagreement regarding the denial of payment or reimbursement of unauthorized medical expense.

The Tampa VAMC has not responded to the Veteran's notice of disagreement, to include issuing a statement of the case regarding this issue. Under these circumstances, the Board is obliged to remand this issue to the AOJ for the issuance of a statement of the case. Stegall V West, 11 VET. App. 268 (1998); Manlincon V. West, 12 Vet. App. 238, 240-41 (1999).

Accordingly, the case is REMANDED for the following action:

1. *The AOJ must take appropriate action and issue a statement of the case that addresses the issue of entitlement to payment or reimbursement of unauthorized medical expenses. The Veteran should be informed that, in order to perfect an appeal of this issue to the Board, he must file a timely and adequate substantive appeal following the issuance of the statement of the case. This issue need not be returned to the Board unless appellate review is otherwise*

perfected. The Veteran has the right to submit additional evidence and argument on the matter the Board has remanded. Kutscherousky V. West, 12 Vet. App. 369 (1999).

This claim must be afforded expeditious treatment. The law requires that all claims that are remanded by the Board or by the United States Court of Appeals for Veterans Claims for additional development or other appropriate action must be handled in an expeditious manner. See 38 U.S. C.A. 5109 B, 7112 (West 2014)

Under 38 U.S.C.A. 7252 (West 2014), only a decision of the Board of Veterans' Appeals is appealable to the United States Court of Appeals for Veterans Claims. This remand is in the nature of a preliminary order and does not constitute a decision of the Board on the merits of your appeal. 38 C.F.R. 20. 1100(b) (2015).

Signed by:

Thomas J. Dannaher

Veterans Law Judge, Board of Veterans' Appeals

Well there it is. With ten years of college education and a Ph. D in research it was difficult to interrupt or fully understand this letter which was common in most responses that were received from them. I couldn't help but wonder about those who were unfortunate and had less of an education. Most response letters are overwhelming to them?

Their response letters kept referring to the same ole same ole: unauthorized medical expenses incurred by his own private hospitalization at Bartow Regional Medical Center. Yet the Veterans Hospital had created the life-threatening situation that necessitated me, the veteran, being admitted to the nearest emergency room.

***The understanding* of the above letter was:** The Veterans Administration was much slower in making a decision than the law allowed. A more expedited process was required. According to the remand the Veterans Administration had to respond at a faster pace. Maybe a lawyer should be involved to fully understand their "mumbo-jumbo."

At times, I would receive a letter from the Veterans Administration that gave me hope, then those hopes would be dashed with the next letter. Soon hope would fade and be replaced with frustration. This vicious cycle seemed to have no end.

Twice Ambushed

Department of Veterans Affairs

July 10, 2017

Dear Mr. Pemberton:

*We are returning your appeal to the Board of Veterans'
Appeals for disposition. This means that your records
are being transferred to Washington, DC, so that the
Board can reach a decision on your appeal.*

*Appeals are considered by the Board as promptly as
possible, in docket order. Your appeal retains the
docket number that it received when it was originally
certified to the Board. Once an appeal has reached the
Board, it usually takes several months to review it. The
time it takes to complete the appellate review process
will vary depending upon the current caseload at the
Board.*

*You should submit any further correspondence on your
case directly to the Board. As soon as the decision is
made, the Board will notify you.*

Thank you for your service

VA Regional Office

The last response that was received from the Veterans Administration concerning this claim was in January 2018. It was another denial. This letter contained an oddity. It stated that they had sent a copy of the denial to the Disabled American Veterans Organization. It was sent there because I had been represented by the DAV at the hearing. The Board was represented by an attorney whose name is, K. Kovarovic..

Interesting, the Board was represented by an attorney, whom adequately represented the Veterans Administration. However, If the DAV had represented me, then surely, I was presented with inadequate representation since no one from the DAV ever interviewed me. Without a one-on-one interview, whether it be in person or by phone, it would be impossible to adequately represent me.

Confusing issue - It is confusing that an assigned representative from a Veterans Service Organization, who is supposed to represent a claimant, never makes any contact with the claimant. The question is, if someone is representing a person how is it possible without a consultation with the one being represented?

Many veterans, in their attempt to steer the claimant in the right direction, have suggested that a Veterans Organization be involved. This has been tried and as of this date not one has put much effort in resolving this claim.

Twice Ambushed

Last correspondence from the VA - The last correspondence received from the Veterans Administration is dated January 14, 2018. My first claim for a medical disability was originally made in 1973. Using an elementary addition scale that adds up to forty-four years and the claim is still active. They have done a very good job of stalling, destroying records, and in general just using delay tactics.

Department of Veterans Affairs
Board of Veterans' Appeals
Washington DC 20038

Date: 09/14/17

Dear Appellant:

Your appeal has been returned to the Board of Veterans' (Board) and has resumed its place on the docket.

The Boards database reflects that you have appointed a Veterans Service Organization to represent you. As such, your representative has requested to review your file and prepare written argument on your behalf prior to the Board making a determination. The Board cannot consider your appeal until this review is completed.

Since your appeal was previously remanded for additional development, please be assured that it will be handled expeditiously. Although we make every effort to decide your appeal as quickly as possible, the time needed to render a decision can vary depending on a number of factors, including the amount of time spent by your representative in review of your appeal as well as the complexity of your appeal.

Any questions about factual or legal matters involved in your appeal should be directed to your representative. You may contact the Board at (800) 923-8387 from 8:00 a.m. to 4:30 p.m. eastern time, Monday through Friday, or via fax at (202) 495-6803.

Sincerely

Donnie R. Hachey

Chief Counsel for Operations

For further research for this book I Googled "Veteran Horror Stories." With great disbelief, one story after another was discovered of veteran's in their plight with the Veterans Administration.

 Listed are a few of the stories:

"Privacy Violation Rising at Veterans Affairs Medical Facilities" www.google.com ***(ProPublica's)***

December 30, 2015

By: Annie Waldman & Charles Ornstein

 When Anthony McCann opened a thick manila envelope from the Department of Veterans Affairs last year, he expected to find his own medical records inside. Instead, he found over 250 pages of deeply revealing personal information on another veteran's mental health. McCann stated, "It had everything about him, and I could have done anything with it."

This wasn't the first time McCann had received medical records belonging to another veteran. A ProPublica analysis shows that employees and contractors at VA medical centers, clinics, pharmacies and benefit centers commit thousands of privacy violations each year and have racked up more than 10,000 such incidents since 2011.
The breaches range from inadvertent mistakes, such as sending documents or prescriptions to the

wrong people, to employees' intentional snooping and theft of data. Not all concern medical treatment; some involve data on benefits and compensation.[2]

"VA hiding documents on veteran deaths in Florida"

In Florida, delays in treatment likely contributed to five deaths and nine other injuries according to documents released to the Tampa Tribune. The deaths were rumored to be linked to two hospitals, the James A. Haley Veterans' in Tampa and the C.W. "Bill Young" VA Medical Center. Nationwide, at least nineteen veteran deaths have been linked to delays. At least 63 other veterans suffered injuries. According to the documents released, the deaths were the result of delayed endoscopy tests.

It was stated that Senator Bill Nelson should be focusing on whether or not the treatment in the hospital contributed to the deaths. Instead, Senator Nelson seemed to be focused on whether or not the veterans died in VA hospitals in question.

More information was sought regarding the deaths. However, the VA is now blocking any further release of information since it is currently locked in a fight with the Tribune over further document releases. (Source: The Tampa Tribune)[3]

Twice Ambushed

"Lie, Delay and Deny Until They Die:
How Veterans are treated by the VBA"

This is the working mantra of the Veterans Benefits Administration (VBA). After reading the latest report from the Office of the Inspector General, this is made blatantly clear. The mantra has long been rumored among veterans but, with all the information coming from the series of joint committee hearings, it has proven to be the truth.

The report is titled, "Veterans Benefits Administration: Review of the Special Initiative To Process Rating Claims Pending Over Two Years."

This document describes an agency that moved claims out of pending status to inflate their numbers of claims completed by 12 percent. It reports that 32 percent, nearly a third of the claims the IG tracked, contained errors in rating the veteran's disability. There was an estimated 17,600 out of 56,500 claims, that is about 31 percent, inaccurately processed resulting in over 40 million dollars in incorrect payments.

Meanwhile, the VBA reports an over 90 percent in rating disability claims and has reduced the backlog by more than half. Here is how they are able to perform this magic trick. The VBA is clearing the backlog by denying claims, turning the claim into an appeal, which is no longer counted as a pending claim. In their own words, according to a Senate Committee on Veteran Affairs press release. The VBA "misrepresented the actual workload of pending claims and its progress toward eliminating the overall claims backlog." As a result, the appeals workload "has continued to grow at an alarming rate."

The author of this article stated, "he was a veteran who had been treated for PTSD and depression for over a year. They were good at getting the assessment and treated as soon as the schedule allowed. A claim was filed, and it took a year for the claim to be denied. The reason for denial was for "lack of medical evidence." The VA had treated this condition yet denied a claim for an injury which was being treated by the Veteran's Hospital.

What a quandary! The Veterans Health Administration says the injury was probably the result of service during the Persian Gulf War. The Veteran's Benefit Administration said that there was no injury and if there was one, it was not the result of being in a war zone because they have no record of one. "But you can appeal" they pointed out.

"What the VA has created is an industry that grinds along on the misery of injured veterans. The author of this article stated, "I am one of the lucky ones because they haven't killed me yet and I can still appeal."

The system has been warped to benefit the bureaucrats who work within and alongside the VA. The agency spends millions on a computer system that ends up using decade old technology and can't communicate with other agency's computers. That is why we get reports of VA facilities spending millions on office equipment, appliances and decorations but not a penny on feedback surveys from the veterans that are treated.[4]

(This article was written by Mark Rogers, July 24, 2014 for the Indian Country Media Network. He served in the U.S. Army Reserves Medical Corps)

"Veterans say Legitimate claims routinely denied or ignored"

In 1994, Vietnam War Navy Cross recipient Steve Lowery, a retired Marine major from Las Vegas attempted to claim a disability from the Veterans Administration.

In Vietnam, he had been hit in the knee with shrapnel and in the hip with an AK-47 slug. This resulted from a firefight in 1969. The VA benefits office in Reno told him the wounds weren't related to his military service.

The VA disallowed his initial claim because the government's archive agency failed to send his records to Reno. Bewildered by the decision, Lowery provided a copy of his personal medical file in 2010. It has now been in process 14 years. Two years later, his claim was rejected again.

"Lowery is not a story but a reality of how the Department of Veterans Affairs -has failed and still fails to enforce the constitutional rights of our soldiers of war." Said Johnnette Fafard. Fafard lost her

husband, Sgt. Raymond Fafard, in 2013 while waiting a decision from the Veterans Administration.

Retired Navy equipment operator Pete Wallace was informed by the veteran's service manager in Reno that the VA had no record of him being at Fort Hunter Liggett, Calif., where he was injured in 2000.

Wallace said he finds that hard to believe because he submitted copies of his orders, a letter of commendation and his medical records "three or four times." [5]
(Keith Rodgers, Las Vegas Review-Journal, December 13, 2014).

More incompetency

In October 2016, I went to the James A. Haley Veterans Hospital for routine blood work which included an analysis of the urine. This was done as a routine preventive maintenance test.

The analysis indicated a trace of blood in the urine. The urology department ordered an MRI of my kidney.

On December 10, 2016, I received a response on the Urinalysis MRI. It stated:

"I have received your following test: Urinalysis, MRI. Neurosurgery does not suggest that you need surgery for your neck.

Recommendations: results show that there are mild abnormalities that do not require action at this time.

Please follow up as scheduled."

Regards

Lab

Obviously, there was a mistake with this response letter. What did Neurosurgery have to do with a urinalysis MRI? And why did they state that I did not need surgery on my neck as a result of a urinalysis MRI?

I can only guess that when they were responding to my test they were looking at someone else records. It is actually scary that they would mail out a response letter when looking at another one's record.

"V.A. stalemate for army veteran"

WFLA News Channel 8 television in Tampa, Florida assigned Steve Andrews, an investigator reporter, to investigate this particular complaint.

Rich Kinkade of Wimauma, Florida, a community outside Tampa, Florida, was exposed to Agent Orange when he served in the army. In 1970 he ended up in Vietnam, while there he was assigned to an anti-aircraft duster unit, as a medic. His unit provided perimeter defense for field artillery and an American firebase.

Military personnel sent to Vietnam are presumed to have been exposed to the toxic herbicide Agent Orange. Historically heart disease is linked to Agent Orange exposure.

In 2007 Rich took an employment physical for the fire department and flunked the physical. The reason was, "heart disease." He filed a service connected disability claim with the Veterans Administration.

His V.A. file shows that the examiner stated that he had "coronary artery disease." Records indicated that they needed more test, however, they never scheduled any more tests. After a long wait, he wrote a letter asking the V.A, when the confirmatory tests would be scheduled. The V.A. did not respond to his inquiry.

A few months later the V.A. rejected his claim for a service connected disability, stating, "you do not have a diagnosis of heart disease." Rich appealed the denial. He was among the 26,000 veterans waiting for their appeals to be heard in the V.A.'s St. Petersburg region.

In July 2015 VA doctors performed open heart surgery on Rich. He had advanced heart disease. More than a year later, the V.A. still had not decided if Rich had heart disease, even though they had operated on him.

Rich contacted WFLA channel 8 "On your side." WFLA assigned Steve Andrews, a news investigator, to investigate the complaint. After a short investigation, he contacted his congressman, Tom Rooney's office and the V.A. at Bay Pines and told them, "this had to be one of the craziest V.A. stories that he had seen." Both the Congressman's office and the VA promised to look into it. Within a week, the V.A. contacted Rich by phone and told him it had been determined he does in *fact have heart disease.*

The V.A. is claiming the "severe multi-vessel cardiovascular disease" that he suffers from came on suddenly in April 2015. This allows the V.A. to retroactive his claim to 2015. However, he initially was diagnosed in 2010 and he filed a claim in that year. The V.A. seems to be ignoring its own doctor who stated Rich had heart disease in 2010.[6]

(WFLA News Channel 8, "8 on your side tackles V.A. stalemate for army veteran, Steve Andrews, 9-15-16.)

"Pinellas veteran claims 40-year cover-up by Air Force"

Scott Nelms, a former U.S. Air Force pilot called it the "great betrayal." He claims a 40-year cover up may have cost veterans and their families dearly. Nelms said the USAF sprayed significant amounts of the toxic defoliant Agent Orange at bases in Thailand. He accuses the Department of Veterans Affairs of stonewalling veterans who served in Thailand and ignoring the facts about what and when they suffered exposure. He points to a now-declassified 1973 report that said significant use of defoliants occurred on U.S. bases in Thailand. The project CHECO Southeast Asia report "Base Defense in Thailand" also stated defoliants were used inside the perimeter of bases.

Nelms flew about 100 missions out of Thailand, refueling fighter jets and bombers during the Vietnam War. He said his new mission is getting out the word that US veterans who served in Thailand were exposed to significant amounts of Agent Orange.

When Helms left Thailand, he had a skin rash and he saw a civilian doctor when he was released from service, it only took seconds to make a diagnosis. He said the doctor took one look at his hands and said, "you've been exposed to toxic industrial chemicals."

The rash spread over all of Helms' body and lasted for seven years. He eventually contacted the VA and asked if he had been exposed to Agent Orange. When he told the lady at the VA that he had been stationed in Thailand her reply was, "Oh no, we never sprayed it in Thailand, so it must be something else."

In Congressional hearings, Congress continued to deny that Agent Orange was used in Thailand until the 1973 report on "Project CHECO" was declassified.

The Congressional Research Service provided members with a 2014 report called "Veterans Exposed to Agent Orange: Legislative History, Litigation, and Current Issues." This report does not mention whatsoever the use of Agent Orange in Thailand.

Nelms said that today he is on a different mission. Instead of flying KC 135's he is working to ensure Thailand veterans are treated equitably by the VA. He said, "the sad thing is that many vets that did have diseases that were affected by Agent Orange have passed, their kids have no idea what went on.[7]

(WFLA News Channel 8, Pinellas veteran claims 40-year cover-up by Air Force, Steve Andrews Investigator Reporter 12-21-2016)

Twice Ambushed

WFLA News Channel 8 said they would continue digging deeper into issues that impact our veterans. As a follow-up on stories involving vets they did another segment called "Delay, Deny Until They Die" on December 31, 2016.

"Veterans Unload on Congressman Crist"

In a meeting with Congressman Charlie Crist (D- St. Petersburg, Florida) veterans told him to leave his politics at the door – they were ready to talk meat and potatoes.

They met with the lawmaker at the American Legion Post 273 in Madeira Beach, Florida. Congressman Crist listened, took notes and received an earful.

Such topics as healthcare, transitioning from active duty to retirement, and the delay, deny and cover-up that is so common in the Veterans Administration.

One veteran told the Congressman that he goes to a private doctor because of the treatment at the VA Hospital. He said he told the doctors at the VA that through an outside doctor he was told that he needed back surgery. His primary doctor at the VA advised not to have the surgery that he would continue to treat it with pain pills.

Beverly Young, the widow of former Congressman Bill Young (Florida) gave Congressman Crist some advice. She told him the VA is too big to fix and suggested Crist meet with the new V.A. Secretary David Shulkin to help him fix one hospital at a time, starting with Bay Pines. "Put it under a glass dome and fix every problem that they find there on a one-to-one basis and use that hospital as an example that the V.A. can be fixed," said Young.[8]

The VA operates a large number of sites:

1233 Health care facilities and clinics
168 Medical centers
1053 Outpatient sites

(WFLA Channel 8, Veterans unload on Congressman Crist, Steve Andrews, Investigating reporter, 4-21-17)

The results are always the same, pass the buck, make promises and forget them, and hope the veteran will eventually go away through death.

Veteran discrimination – A non- combat veteran who goes to the VA medical facility for medical treatment and does not meet the financial criteria is charged large co-payments. All non-combat veterans who are admitted to the health care facilities are admitted on an income-based criteria. The co-payment that is charged is determined on the household income and number of family members living in the same household. A family of two must have an annual income no more than $38,000.00 to escape large co-payment on each visit. If the veteran's income exceeds the limited amount then a one-night stay in the veteran's hospital will cost the veteran a minimum of $1300.00 in a co-payment. That expense does not include the following: time driving the distance to a veteran's hospital, fuel and food plus a nice fat co-payment for each visit to see a doctor. The co-payment to see their primary care doctor is usually from $50.00 to $75.00.

Veterans that have an income less than thirty-eight thousand for a family of two receive medical treatment free and in many cases, they receive travel pay to travel to the VA hospital. Partiality should not be imposed simply because some earn more money than others.

Each veteran chose to serve their country and in doing so placed their life in danger. There is no status symbol just because one earns more than another one.

I am not a combat veteran; however, I was in the army during the Viet-Nam war and the "Cold War." I was just a lucky one. Those who served in a non-combat role supported those who were on the front lines. Without the support soldier there would be a non-effective combat soldier. The "Cold War" included keeping the peace in Europe and restricting Communism from expanding in that part of the world.

Where is the fairness here? Soldiers are penalized for coming home and deciding they want to make a decent living for their families.

Chapter Fifteen: Memphis

Donovan Slack, a reporter for USA Today has done several investigative stories on the conditions that affect the health care of our veterans. Below is a couple of examples of his investigative work.

"VA hired workers with revoked medical licenses"

The Department of Veterans Affairs allowed its hospitals across the country to hire health care providers with revoked medical licenses for at least 15 years in violation of federal law, a USA Today investigation found.

The VA issued national guidelines in 2002 giving hospitals discretion to hire clinicians after "prior consideration of all relevant facts surrounding" any revocations and as long as they still had a license in one state.

A federal law passed in 1999 bars the VA from employing any health care worker whose license has been yanked by any state.

Hospital officials at the VA in Iowa City relied on the illegal guidance this year to hire neurosurgeon John Henry Schneider, who revealed in his application that he had numerous malpractice claims and settlements and Wyoming had revoked his license after a patient died. He still had a license in Montana.

The VA moved to fire Schneider Nov. 29 after inquiries about his case from USA Today. He resigned instead. The VA said at the time that Iowa City hospital officials received "incorrect guidance" green-lighting his hiring in April. The agency conceded this week that it was national policy.

VA Secretary David Shulkin said in an interview that he ordered the rewriting of the guidelines and launched a nationwide review to identify and remove any other health care workers with revoked licenses. "It's very clear to me that our job is to have the best quality doctors that we can provide to take care of our veterans, and that's going to be our policy," he said.

Shulkin said health care providers with sanctions against their medical licenses short of revocation, suspensions, or reprimands will be reviewed to ensure they provide quality care to veterans at the VA.

The USA Today investigation found that in addition to hiring Schneider, VA hospitals knowingly hired other health care providers with license penalties. In some cases, they went on to harm veterans.

A VA hospital in Oklahoma hired a psychiatrist sanctioned for sexual misconduct who slept with a VA patient.

The VA in Tomah, Wis., hired a psychiatrist disciplined for medication violations who overprescribed narcotics to veterans. A Louisiana VA clinic hired a psychologist with felony convictions. The VA fired him after determining he was a "direct threat to others" and the VA's mission.

USA Today reported that the malpractice claims against Schneider included cases alleging he made surgical mistakes that left patients maimed, paralyzed or dead and that his veteran patients in Iowa suffered complications. One of those patients, Richard Joseph Hopkins, 65, died from infection in August after four brain surgeries by Schneider in a span of four weeks.

Hopkin's' daughter Amy McIntire, told USA Today she is furious Schneider was hired and floored by the national policy that allowed it.

"I'm appalled by the ineptitude at the VA," said McIntire, a registered nurse who noted that an agency so large has numerous staffers to write policies and ensure they comply with federal law. "For it just to be ignored, it's crazy."

Schneider denied in an interview that he provided substandard care and blamed poor patient outcomes on other providers or unfortunate complications that can occur in neurosurgery

A group of 14 senators from both parties wrote VA Secretary David Shulkin asking about hiring and oversight of health care workers with known histories of malpractice and license discipline. That followed letters from Montana Democratic Sen. Jon Tester and Iowa Republican Sens. Joni Ernst and Chuck Grassley, who said it was "unacceptable that it was only as a result of USA TODAY's report that the VA determined that hiring this neurosurgeon was illegal.

Later, 31 members of the House of Representatives fired off letters to the VA secretary expressing "extreme concern."

"The hiring of doctors who have had their medical licensees revoked in any state is already prohibited," wrote 30 of the lawmakers, including members of the Veterans Affairs Committee.

Rep. Mike Coffman, R-Colo., demanded in his own letter that Shulkin launch a nationwide review to identify other VA health care workers with malpractice complaints and settlements or sanctions for poor care.

(Donovan Slack, USA TODAY "VA hired workers with revoked medical licenses" December 22-25, 2017, P. — 1, 2A.)

Donovan Slack, USA Today, and Jake Lowary, USA Today Network, did an investigative story on the conditions at the VA hospital in Memphis, Tennessee. They discovered a place that they described as a "House of horrors." The following is what they discovered:

Chapter Fifteen: Memphis

VA hospital in Memphis called a "House of Horrors."

A veteran with diabetes and poor circulation checked into the Memphis VA Medical Center for a scan and possible repair of blood vessels in his right leg last year, but he ended up with a piece of plastic packaging that VA providers had mistakenly embedded in a critical artery.

Doctors didn't discover 10 inches of tubing – used by manufacturers to protect catheters during shipping and handling, until the veteran had to have the leg amputated three weeks later.

When they cut into his leg, they found a three- inch segment, and after the procedure, they found an additional 7 inches in the amputated limb.

The error is one of a litany of patient safety issues at the Memphis hospital in recent years chronicled in a trove of internal documents obtained by the USA TODAY Network that provide a revealing glimpse of one of the worst of 168 VA hospitals in the country.

The hospital is one of only four on which the VA's top health official, acting Under Secretary for Health Poonam Alaigh' requested weekly briefings, according to the documents.

The Memphis VA scores only one out of five stars in the agency's quality-of-care rankings and the documents show reports of threats to patient safety at the hospital soared to more than 1000 last year, up from 700 the year before. Are veterans receiving quality care?

Among the other serious incidents investigated in 2016: The medical center mishandled a tissue sample resulting in a repeat biopsy, a provider perforated a patient's colon during a colonoscopy, and a patient with abdominal pain and blood in his urine waited two hours in the emergency room before leaving for another hospital where the patient "was deemed urgent and seen immediately."

According to VA statistics, the hospital is among the worst in the country for patient safety and in patient outcomes. Death rates following acute care or pneumonia treatment also are among the worst of any of the agency's medical centers.

The VA quietly removed an array of top managers at the hospital in recent weeks, including the chiefs of surgery, anesthesiology, and research, according to internal documents.

In response to inquiries from USA Today, a spokesman for VA Secretary David Shulkin said a new director took over in May and did a top to bottom review of the facility. VA press secretary Curt Cashour said the staff changes are the result of that review, which found problems in surgery, research, nursing, engineering, and human resources.

He said Shulkin, who took over as secretary in February, has made it a priority to quickly identify and address vulnerabilities across the VA system.

"When we determine facilities need extra attention, such as those in Memphis and Marion, Ill., they are receiving it," Cashour said. "And we are not hesitating to take swift accountability actions when warranted."

- Marion, Ill., where significant declines in patient safety culture and reported deaths prompted an investigation earlier this year.
- Washington, D.C., where investigators found surgical shortfalls earlier this year that placed veterans in imminent danger.
- Manchester, N.H., where *the Boston Globe* revealed dangerous conditions in July, in a fly-infested operating room and canceled surgeries.

They may represent a small sliver of the VA's 168 hospitals across the nation, but the stakes are high for the thousands of veterans reliant on them.

Mary Davis says she knows first-hand just how bad care can be at the Memphis VA, and how tragic the consequences.

After her husband, Vietnam veteran Charles Davis, collapsed on the kitchen floor in their Atoka, Tenn. home in 2015, an MRI scan showed he had a tumor in his neck. She said when she asked doctors to check a scan taken at the VA the previous year, they found the tumor had been visible, but VA clinicians had failed to diagnosis it.

By the time they caught it, the tumor had damaged his spine and he is now paralyzed. "They should have caught it" she told USA Today. "I am totally 100% disappointed in the care."

Twice Ambushed

The Memphis VA has faced a seemly intractable cascade of problems for years. In 2012, investigators concluded veterans had endured serious treatment delays at the hospital. The emergency department was so overcrowded, patients were left on stretchers in hallways, some as long as 14 hours and others left without ever being seen.

A year later, they found delays in processing "urgent laboratory tests" and that patients had died in the emergency room. One received a medication for which the patient had a known drug allergy, another wasn't monitored after receiving multiple sedating medications, and a third with high blood pressure suffered a bleed in the brain, again after inadequate monitoring.

In 2014, employees started blowing the whistle on continuing lapses, from neglected medical records to contaminated medical equipment. A video in 2015 purported showed an empty nurse' station in the critical spine cord wing.

VA officials ousted the hospital director amid "underperformance" issues in February 2016, but the problems continued. In May 2016, OSHA, which monitors citations to the hospital, issued a citation for improper disposal of human tissue.

A *"House of Horrors"* – "It's a house of horrors," said Sean Higgins, a former logistics technician at the hospital.

Cashour, the VA press secretary, said the agency is continuing to investigate problems discovered in the top-to-bottom review conducted in recent months, including shortfalls in the surgical department.

He said the VA wants to "understand how these problems developed, and hold accountable those responsible.

Rep. Phil Roe, R-Tenn. Chairman, of the House Veterans Affairs Committee, said he is "outraged" by the ongoing issues at the Memphis VA. His staff has been investigating the hospital since January when videos showed two staff members allegedly abusing a patient.

Roe said, "I'm disappointed and outraged by the many failures at the Memphis VA medical center, particularly the allegations regarding patient safety" in a statement. "This is unacceptable, plain and simple. [9]

After extended research, it appears that incompetence is a common visitor at many veteran's hospitals. There are too many veterans that are falling through the cracks in their health care in these facilities. The task of removing the incompetent workers falls into the hands of congress. Congress has been slack in the past with routing out those who are not doing their job, therefore, the President of the United States should declare this an emergency situation.

Chapter Sixteen: Re-Connected

Renewed VA Association - By May 2017, I had moved on and was going to a private cardiologist in Lakeland, Florida. I had been seeing a VA assigned primary care doctor only once a year. These appointments were to keep my healthcare privileges active. Except for visits to the primary care I had no contact with the doctors at the James A. Haley Veterans Hospital for several years.

Because of a pacemaker, I had to see the Lakeland cardiologist every three or four months. A representative of Medtron, the pacemaker company which had provided my pacemaker, would meet me at this cardiologist's office and do an interrogation on my pacemaker.

Summer of 2017 – Toward the end of May, I received a phone call from the Cardiac Care Unit at James A. Haley Hospital. A nurse practitioner reported they had received my last "wireless" transmission and there was a problem with my pacemaker. An appointment was made for me to go into the cardiac care unit, the next morning.

Upon arriving at the appointment, the next morning, some tests were run. It was discovered that a lead wire had come lose in my pacemaker. The lose wire caused the pacemaker to malfunction. Since its function was to keep my heart beating, the news sounded serious.

Dr. Raymond Cutro, who is the director of the Electrophysiology lab, introduced himself and said he would be the attending physician. The doctor explained what was happening and the treatment plan. It required surgery to go into my heart and extract two lead wires and replace my pacemaker. The pacemaker would be replaced with a combination pacemaker and defibrillator.

Dr. Cutro appeared very knowledgeable and passionate. As I listened to him explain the procedure I felt that Dr. Cutro had an interest in my well-being. The doctor informed me that it was a very risky surgery. However, he said that if surgery was not done soon I would die. I was again admitted into the James A. Haley Veterans Hospital.

The thoughts of the botched removal of the sheath (that nearly killed me) was still fresh on my mind even though it had taken place over seven years ago. I told Dr. Cutro that I was apprehensive because of what had happened the last time as a patient at James A. Haley Hospital.

Dr. Cutro assured me that things had gotten better over the last few years. A rapport developed and my confidence level increased.

With the risk level of the surgery being so high, Dr. Cutro had me transferred to the Pepin Heart Institute at the Florida Hospital in Tampa. He said if anything went wrong the Pepin Heart Institute would be more prepared to handle an emergency. This was a comforting feeling because Florida Hospital has a reputation for being an excellent heart hospital in Tampa.

The four-hour surgical procedure was a success. It was performed by Dr. Cutro from the VA hospital and a team of advisors at the Florida Hospital.

Recovery took another five days and as usual it was a bit uncomfortable. I was sent home with an appointment to return in three-weeks for a check-up. Dr. Cutro talked to me about the atrial fibrillation that I was experiencing. After consultation, the doctor decided that a cardioversion may help the situation. This was a procedure where the heart was stopped and re-started. In July, 2017 the procedure was done as an outpatient and it went well. Dr. Cutro was the attending surgeon on this procedure. After the cardioversion my heart was back in rhythm. This was great news since the atrial fibrillation had been a problem for five years.

During this time, I recognized that another problem with my heart existed. I believed an artery was clogged. This was discussed with Dr. Cutro and he agreed that a heart cath should be scheduled. Three weeks after the cardioversion Dr. Cutro scheduled a heart catherization and this was to be done as an in-patient surgery.

It was at this time that I was introduced to Dr. Reddy, a cardiologist in the heart cath lab. Dr. Reddy was assigned to do this procedure. As with Dr. Cutro, I established a rapport with Dr. Reddy and I came to really trust these two doctors. I felt that God had surely initiated my meeting these doctors.

Chapter Sixteen: Re-Connected

After the heart cath procedure, Dr. Reddy came to my room and informed me that a stent in an artery had clogged and blood flow was at 15%. He had solved the problem by doing an angioplasty. However, with so many procedures the arteries walls had become thin. Should a future problem arise that required a heart catherization it could not be done. The next time would require open heart surgery (Bi-pass surgery).

Life change suggested – Dr. Reddy said there was a plan "B". This plan would require a life change in my eating habits. He recommended a change that at first seemed very drastic. This plan was, "no meat, cheese or eggs." All my adult life I was person who believed that if I did not have meat with a meal, then there had been no meal. However, By-pass surgery was not on my "want to-do list." Dr. Reddy asked me to commit to a diet free of meat, cheese and eggs for at least three-months. I readily promised that I would make that commitment. Dr. Reddy probably thought, "that was too easy, he won't stick with it." I think I fooled both Dr. Reddy and myself. As of this writing I have been a vegetarian for eighteen months and the results have been unbelievable.

About two years earlier I was praying and had asked God to heal me of diabetes. Within seconds, I believe the Holy Spirit responded and said, "I have done my part, you need to do your part." I knew immediately the Holy Spirit was speaking to my excess weight. There needed to be a change in my eating habits. I had known what I needed to do but never seemed to have the discipline to do it. With the possibility of open-heart surgery in my near future, I have motivation. Life has been different with the new diet change. I have been without meat for over a year and a half yet I have had no meat craving, surly God has been with me.

Both my wife and I are now eating "Heart heathy" and continue to lose weight. My diabetes is much more manageable, and I am taking a fraction of the insulin that I use to take. An echo gram showed that my heart, which previously was pumping at 30%, is now back to normal. We both exercise for over an hour each day and both of us feel much younger.

Old games for the VA - After leaving the VA hospital a bill was sent to me for $1800.00. Our household income did not meet what the VA allowed for non-copayment.

Enclosed with the bill was a letter explaining that we could request a compromise. Since there was a possibility that they would approve a compromise I filled out the necessary forms and mailed them to the address listed. Every form requires four to six weeks to receive a decision. This was no exception. About six weeks later I received a denial on my request. However, another enclosed letter stated that I could apply for a payment plan. Again, I filled out the necessary forms and mailed them to the address listed. Six weeks later, an approval letter for a payment plan arrived. It stated I could pay a minimum of fifty-dollars a month. Our plan was to pay $800.00 on the first payment and $500.00 the next two months. This would eliminate the debt completely within three months.

Payment on the bill goes to Atlanta, Georgia. The request form for a payment plan goes to Orlando, Florida.

We mailed a check for the first $795.30 and the next month we waited for the next bill to arrive. The usual date for the bill came and went and we did not receive a bill.

A few days later a letter arrived from a federal collection agency (Treasury's Debt Management Service). This letter requested that I call them to discuss payment options on a late debt.

My wife called the number on the letter and a lady answered the phone. She asked the lady to explain why we had received such a letter. The lady stated she had no authority to discuss the account. However, she did say that an additional 30% of the bill had been added for collection service. It was no longer $1800.00, now it was $2250.00 because of the 30% added. The $795.30 check had not been deducted from the account even though it had been processed and paid by our bank three weeks earlier.

My wife asked for a phone number of someone who could answer her questions. She was given another phone number and when my wife dialed that number a gentleman answered the phone. She asked why our account had been turned over for collection and was not given credit for the payment that she had paid.

Twice Ambushed

The man on the other end of the line said that he did not have an answer to our question. Before the day was over at least a half-dozen calls were made before being routed to someone who said they could help.

The last person that she was routed to was asked why the payment of $795.30 had not been applied to the account? The second question was, why had they referred the account to a collection agency? This person did not have an answer to those questions either. However, he did say they would send back the payment of $795.30 to us but was subtracting a 30% fee. Again, we asked, how could they charge the fee. He said, "it was because it had been sent to a collection agency. When asked, how could they charge a 30% fee when the payment was never applied to the account, we received their standard answer "that's the way we do it." Eventually the payment was returned without any explanation.

It was quite clear that within the Veterans Administration the left hand does not know what the right hand is doing.

One of America's greatest misconception: "All veterans receive free health care" This is far from the truth – only those who are combat veterans or have a very low income receive free health care.

Chapter Seventeen: Conclusion

The Veterans Administration is like a giant monster without anyone at the helm. It goes from one veteran to another and swallows them up. After it gets its fill, a few veterans will be given some service. That is, until it decides to chew up a few more veterans. The system is very problematic, and no one seems to have the authority to resolve any of the problems. There isn't any problem-solving department head. The departments that do function, the right hand does not know what the left hand is doing. Personal experience and research implicates the system as being one big mess.

The problems have been ongoing for several years and the politicians apply band-aids year after year. Nothing credible has changed over the last several years. The system is so ineffective that men and women who have given so much come home to empty promises. Many veterans end up dying at the hands of the Veterans Administration.

America's prized possession - The veteran is recognized as America's prized possession, yet they are treated so badly by the very organization that is supposed to help them. It is past time for America to show their appreciation in tangible ways. It is nice to "thank a vet" but from the vet's prospective it is better to be shown than told.

Rescued dogs and cats – A few days ago, there was a news report on the 6 O'clock News in Tampa, Florida where the American Animal Association rescued several dogs from a meat packing plant in Korea. Some of the dogs were shipped to the ASPC in Tampa. It appears that dogs are butchered and served for meals in Korea. It was a wonderful thing that those dogs were rescued, however, why give animals greater aid and comfort than our sick and maimed veterans. After-all, dogs are dogs and veterans are human beings?

Protest after protest in favor of: Cats, dogs, turtles, turtle eggs, manatees, birds, bird nests, women rights, perceived injustices, and trees take place day after day. However, veterans who put their life on hold for long periods of time seems to be less significant than other things which are entitled to benefits that veterans find it difficult to obtain.

Recently I heard a news report that Americans spend over ten billion dollars a year to feed, provide medical care and to pamper their pets.

Has America's value of keeping our country free changed? Certainly, the Veterans Administration is not a priority to incumbent and incoming politicians. If we are going to continue to live in a country that enjoys its freedom and democracy, our veterans need to be treated better than the pets.

America without it's "freedom fighters." - With an all-volunteer military, some politicians seem to believe that when one volunteers for military life they deserve what happens to them.

Americans should thank God for the ones who

volunteer to safeguard our freedom. It is un-imaginable what a society, such as ours, would be like without our "Protectors." Without them, chaos would be maximized. This includes both the military and America's police force.

The crack in our social system is getting larger and larger. Many people do not respect the flag and insist on protesting our American ways by refusing to stand for the National anthem. There is an all-out assault against the police. At times, our schools have become war zones. The crime has reached an all-time high. If things continue as they are it may reach the point of having to hire professional body guards to go shopping.

Many of the older citizens are asking, "What is this country coming to?" It is a great question and it demands an answer.

The ancient Roman Empire, the greatest in history, experienced its decline from within. A foreign enemy was never able to conquer that great empire, however, internal turmoil did what a foreign enemy was not able to do. Will America replicate that great Roman Empire?

Unless the American people demand that our politicians, government officials and people in-charge turn this ship around, our society is doomed. What is good, and right is being called bad and what is evil is being called good.

Twice Ambushed

"Woe to those who call good evil and evil good, who put darkness for light and light for darkness, who put bitter for sweet and sweet for bitter." **Isa. 5:20**

America has been warned, however, history tells us that humans do not learn from history. The Old Testament gives us the first historical insight into human learning skills.

Over the years the assistance of politicians and government official have been sought, however, no one responded in a favorable way. Below is a list of names that was solicited to assist in resolving this situation. The first list are names of people who responded to my request for assistance. Each response was cordial and they "thanked" me for allowing them to help. The problem was that this veteran did not receive any help.

Enclosures: Response Letters received from:

U.S. Senator Bill Nelson (D)
Florida
Washington, D.C.

U.S. Congressman Adam Putnam (R)
12th District, Florida
Washington, D.C.

U.S. Congressman Dennis Ross (R)
15th District, Florida
Washington, D.C.

Disabled American Veterans
National Service Office
St. Petersburg, Florida

Department of Veterans Affairs
St. Petersburg, Florida

National Personnel Records Center
St. Louis, Mo.

Board of Veterans Appeals
Washington, D.C.

***Elected officials where requests for assistance were sent and no response was ever received.**

U. S. Senator Vern Buchanan (R) Florida
Washington, D.C.

U.S. Senator Mitch McConnell (R) Kentucky
Washington, D.C.

Secretary of the Army
Washington, D.C.

U.S. Senator Marco Rubio (R) Florida
Orlando Field Office
Orlando, Fl.

References

[1] Dayton Daily News, 'Veteran Whose Records Were Missing Sues Dayton VA., Barrie Barber Staff Writer, Sept.15, 2013.

[2] www. google .com, Propublica, Anne Waldman 7 Charles Ornstein, December 30, 2015.

[3] Tampa Tribune, Tampa, Florida, "VA hiding Documents on Veterans Deaths in Florida."

[4] Indian Country Media Network, "Lie and Deny Until They Die: How Veterans are treated" Mark Rodgers, July 24, 2014.

[5] Los Vegas Review-Journal, "Veterans Say Legitimate Claims Routinely Denied or Ignored," Keith Rodgers, December 13, 2014.

[6] WFLA News Channel 8, Tampa, Fla., "8 on your side" "VA Stalemate for Army Vet." Steve Andrews, Sept. 15,2016.

[7] WFLA News Channel 8, Tampa, Fla., "Pinellas Veteran Claims 40-Year Cover-up." Steve Andrews Investigative reporter, Dec. 21, 2016.

[8] WFLA News Channel 8, Tampa, Fla., "Veterans Unload on Congressman Crist," Steve Andrews Investigative Reporter, April 21, 2017.

[9] USA Today, "VA Hospital in Memphis called a "House of Horror," Donovan Slack & Jake Lowary, Sept., 11 2017, P. 1-1.

<u>**Other books written by Dr. Charles L. Pemberton**</u>

All books can be ordered through Amazon.com or from the author.

"Lord Tell Me How" *(Publisher, Carlton Press, New York, New York)*

"Contaminated Mind" *(Publisher, CreateSpace, Columbia, South Carolina)*

"Faith or Insanity, You Decide," *(Publisher, CreateSpace, Columbia, South Carolina)*

"Profile of an American Education" *(Publisher, CreateSpace, Columbia, South Carolina)*

9 781727 136258